Robert M Newman

OCCULT ILLUSTRATED DICTIONARY

HARVEY DAY

KAYE & WARD · LONDON
OXFORD UNIVERSITY PRESS
NEW YORK

First published in Great Britain by
Kaye & Ward Ltd,
21 New Street, London EC2M 4NT
1975

First published in the USA by
Oxford University Press Inc.
200 Madison Avenue,
N.Y. 10016, USA
1976

Copyright © Kaye & Ward Ltd 1975

All Rights Reserved. No part of this publication may be reproduced, stored in a retrieval system, or transmitted, in any form or by any means, electronic, mechanical, photocopying, recording or otherwise, without the prior permission of the copyright owner.

ISBN 0 7182 1104 9 (Great Britain)
ISBN 019 519830 1 (USA)
Library of Congress Catalog Card No. 75-21673 (USA)

Printed in Great Britain by
Cox & Wyman Ltd,
London, Fakenham and Reading

FOREWORD

The occult is a vast subject which needs an encyclopedia to do it justice and in a dictionary of this length there are aspects, such as magic and spiritualism, which can only be touched upon. A dictionary is meant primarily to define and act as a book of reference and those whose appetites have been whetted will find all the additional information they require in public libraries or through associations which specialize in such subjects.

More people are now interested in the occult than ever before. During the 18th century most scientists were sure there was nothing beyond the fringe of the material world, but within the last 50 years that belief has been shaken. Spiritualists, theosophists, yogis, the Society for Psychical Research and many others have proved that there exist forces inexplicable by the known laws of science and that there is some kind of existence after physical death. To me there seems to be only the haziest lines of demarcation between the physical, the mental and the spiritual.

Dorchester-on-Thames   HARVEY DAY
Oxon

Note

Cross-referencing of entries is denoted by the symbol °.

ACKNOWLEDGMENTS

The author would like to thank all those who have helped with information, photographs and illustrations, for without their generous assistance the preparation of this book would not have been possible.

In particular he would like to thank: Cyrus D.F. Abayakoon; Mir Bashir; E.H. Carroll-Clark; Wilfred Clark; Margaret Lee of The College of Psychic Studies; Curtis Fuller; M.K. Gandhi; Indra Devi; Noel Jaquin; S.F. Macdonald Lockhart; John Naylor; W.J. Ousby; The Rosicrucian Order (AMORC); The Church of Jesus Christ of Latter-Day Saints; K.J. Thompson; Gordon Turner; Ena Twigg; Dr S. J. Van Pelt; Edward Wagner; and Dr H. Ta'eed of the Bahá'í Church.

The author is also deeply indebted to Ianthe Hoskins of the Theosophical Society; A.H. Wesencraft of the Harry Price Library (London University); The Society For Psychical Research; Charles Harvey of the Astrological Association; Maurice Barbanell of *Psychic News*; The Bodleian Library; *Daily Telegraph*; *Daily Express*; *Scotsman Publications*; The Central Library, Oxford; The Spiritualist Association of Great Britain; The American Society for Psychical Research; The Canadian High Commission; The Australian High Commission; the High Commissioner for Trinidad and Tobago; and the publishers W.H. Allen, Frederick Muller, Colin Smythe and W. Foulsham.

In addition the publishers would like to thank the following for supplying illustrations:

The Australian News and Information Bureau 2, 42, 66; the Trustees of the British Museum 13, 39, 52; *Daily Graphic* 30; Anne Bolt 21, 24; Radio Times Hulton Picture Library 23, 65, 71; The Press Association Ltd, 27; Tom Scott 36; Harry Price Library 38; 49 is from *The Language of the Hand* by Cheiro (Herbert Jenkins, 25th edition, 1900); National Laboratory of Psychical Research 51, 53; London University Library 57; Waddington Playing Card Co. 61; Information Services, Canada House 62; Church of Jesus Christ of Latter-Day Saints 69.

A

Abayakoon, Cyrus D.F. (1912–). Son of one of the hereditary chieftains of Ceylon through whom the British ruled the country. Early in life he was tutored by Buddhist priests, who taught him the little-known art of reading ready-made °horoscopes (*nadi granthams*) inscribed on palm leaves and handed down through the ages, from which it is possible to see past °reincarnations, the present, and the future. On entering government service he read the hands of many with whom he came into contact, saw tribulations, even murders, as well as good fortune and added constantly to his knowledge. Buddhists versed in the lore of °mantras can cure snake-bite by producing the right vibrations and Abayakoon reasoned that it should be possible to cure disease as well by this method. So he studied *mantra-yoga* and has restored to health many who have been given up by orthodox physicians. In India and Ceylon °astrology and °palmistry are sister arts, and he is versed in both. He has made scores of accurate °predictions that have been published and, as early as 1940, he

1. Cyrus Abayakoon

wrote in a newspaper that Haile Selassie would regain his throne and occupy a key position in Africa, and that General de Gaulle would eventually become President of France and wield tremendous power between the ages of 68 and 75, after which both health and influence would decline. Both men were then at the nadir of their fortunes. He also predicted

2. Aborigines of northern Australia in corroboree dress

Churchill's rise to power and fame when he was in the wilderness and, in 1945, predicted that he would lose the General Election. His accurate °predictions about politicians and events would fill many pages: the assassination of Mussolini; the destruction of Hitler; the election victory of Harold Wilson, and his later defeat by Heath; the victory of the Israelis over the Arabs (in 3 days); the assassination of Gandhi; the fall of Krushchev; the assassination of Kennedy and Nixon's rise to be President. In 1971 he foresaw Watergate; °ill. 1.

aborigines (Australian). One of the oldest races on Earth, whose exact origin has never been proved. 'Primitive' anthropologists believe that they descend from an ancient civilization with roots in Java, Ceylon, India and to the west as far as Persia. They had few contacts with Europeans before 1788. Ethnically they belong to a well-defined, specific group, having the soft wavy hair of the European, the wide nose and bone structure of the Negro and the fine pliable skin of the Oriental, so a new category, Australoid, had to be created for them. In some ways their religious beliefs and superstitions may be compared with those of Christianity for they believe that man is composed of three parts: 1. the *atua* or physical body; 2. the *wogai* or °astral body; 3. the *mrsat* or spiritual body. All 3 parts are independent but interrelated. All truth, they say, is in dream-time if only we can draw it out, and all humans emerge from dream-time, where chosen souls are moulded into human form by the 'sky god' and placed in the womb by an earthly father. Death is the result of breaking °taboos and the *wogai* cannot rest till revenged; then the *mrsat* returns to the eternal dream-time. They possess a powerful °sixth sense, can induce °trances during which they travel hundreds of miles in dream-time, and are strongly °telepathic. Tribesmen can send and receive messages over long distances. Music, dancing and ritual play an important part in their lives, and they have a compulsory ceremony which bears a resemblance to the Holy Communion, for it includes the drinking of the sky god's blood and the eating of his body, by initiates. They are probably the most psychically sensitive race on earth. Their *wee-ans* (°witch-doctors) can foretell the future with amazing accuracy by means of °magic stones; °ill. 2 and 41.

abracadabra. A magical word used in the Middle Ages to cure fevers. The earliest instructions for its use were given by Quintus Serenus Sammonicus, a physician who accompanied the Emperor Severus on his expedition to Britain in AD 208. Rows of the word were written, dropping a letter in each successive row to form a triangle, and the paper was tied round the patient's neck with flax, worn for 9 days and then thrown backwards over one shoulder into a stream flowing east. As the word shrank, as symbolized in the triangle, so would the fever be cured. This cure is supposed to have originated with the Jews: 'Ab abr abra abrak abraka abrakal abrakala abrakal abraka abrak abra abr ab' (And the people called unto Moses and Moses prayed to God and the fire abated. May healing come from heaven for all kinds of fever and consumption – heat to N son of N. Amen Amen

```
A B R A C A D A B R A
 A B R A C A D A B R
  A B R A C A D A B
   A B R A C A D A
    A B R A C A D
     A B R A C A
      A B R A C
       A B R A
        A B R
         A B
          A
```

Illustration 3

Amen. Selah Selah Selah). This must be hung round the patient's neck and not looked at for 24 hours; the patient's temperature rises to breaking point, after which it subsides. Another theory is that the word is connected with °Abraxas, a god whose form appeared on charms, rings and °amulets to ward off evil worn by followers of Basilides, leader of a Christian sect which did not believe Christ had been crucified. The letters of the word °Abraxas stand for the seven planets which astrologers of the period believed controlled the destinies of humans; °ill. 3.

Abrams, Dr Albert (?–1922). After qualifying as a doctor, he studied advanced medicine at Heidelberg. When he was in Naples, he watched fascinated while Enrico Caruso, the tenor, flicked a wine-glass with his finger, producing a pure note, then sang the same note to shatter the glass. This stimulated his interest in vibrations, which he eventually used to diagnose and heal. At Heidelberg he studied the work of Professor de Sauer, who was engaged in research on mitogenic radiation. On his return to America, where he taught pathology, Abrams was appointed Head of Stanford University Medical School, where he mastered the art of percussion and, by tapping the body to produce resonating sounds, found clues to disease. One day he switched on an X-ray apparatus, which muffled the resonant note he received while tapping a patient; so he rotated the patient and found that the dulling occurred only when the patient faced east and west, thus proving that there was a relationship between the geomagnetic field and the °vibrations. Later he discovered that a similar effect was produced by a man with a cancerous ulcer on one lip, even though the X-ray machine was not working. After studying hundreds of experiments with patients suffering from various diseases, he became convinced that the nerve fibres in the epigastric region respond to the stimulus of X-rays. This step led ultimately to the invention of a machine called an 'oscilloclast', which he used to diagnose and cure disease. In 1919 he started to teach other physicians how to use it. In 1922 he wrote in the *Physico-Clinical Journal* that it could be used to diagnose diseases in patients thousands of miles from his office. Eventually this led to the development of the Abrams Box, which was further developed and used by George de la Warr, pioneer of °radionics in Britain.

abraxas. Word used by Basilidians (early Christian sect which did not believe Christ had been crucified) and engraved on certain stones which were known as abraxas stones. The letters, in °numerology, add up to 365. Because of this

Basilidians gave the name to 365 orders of °spirits which emanated in succession from the Supreme Being. These orders were supposed to occupy 365 heavens each fashioned like, but inferior to, that above it. The stones often have cabalistic figures engraved on them; °abracadabra; °Kabalah.

absent healing. As the name implies, this is healing without the healer being present and takes a number of forms: the projection of thoughts; the power of prayer; electrical rays sent out by an apparatus specifically designed for that purpose. It is usual for the healer to ask the afflicted person for some small article constantly worn by him so that he can concentrate his thoughts on it. Many remarkable cures – some bordering on the miraculous – have been wrought by this means. Healers claim that cures are effected by °vibrations generated in their bodies; psychologists say that they are brought about by °auto-suggestion; medical men say that they are coincidental and that the conditions would have cleared up anyway in due course; °Christian Science; °faith healing; °psychic healing.

acuto-manzia. °Divination with pins. Thirteen ordinary tacking pins are used, 10 straight and the remainder bent, to represent male, female, and lone. They are shaken gently in cupped hands and then allowed to fall on to a table, the surface of which has been dusted lightly with talcum powder. The reader studies them and gives an assessment of character and predicts future events. Exactly how he does this is a mystery, but it may be assumed that °clairvoyance is used. The outstanding exponent in Europe of this method of divination is Maria Rosa °Donati-Evstigneeff, an Italian, who reads °tarot cards.

Adams, Evangeline (1865–1932). The name under which Mrs George E. Jordan, descendant of John Quincy Adams, sixth President of the United States, practised as an astrological consultant. After studying the subject for several years, she decided to set up professionally at the Windsor Hotel on Fifth Avenue, New York, but before doing so she scrutinized the chart of Warren F. Leland, the proprietor, and told him that he was about to suffer a terrible disaster almost at once. The following afternoon the hotel was burnt to the ground and her future as an astrologer was assured! In 1914 she was arrested for °fortune-telling but decided not to pay the fine imposed. In court she explained how she worked and as a test was given the date of birth of a person unknown to her. She read the °horoscope with uncanny accuracy and, as the subject happened to be the judge's son, he acquitted her and remarked: 'The defendant has raised astrology to the dignity of an exact science.' Her studio at Carnegie Hall was visited by scores of celebrities, among them Edward VII, Caruso and Mary Pickford. J. Pierpont Morgan paid her a handsome retainer to advise him on business, the stock market and politics. In 1930 she began broadcasting three times a week on °astrology and in 3 months received 150,000 letters asking for readings. She predicted the date of her own death and as a result turned down a 21-night lecture tour for the autumn of 1932. When she died, as predicted, the church was crammed with people who wished to be present at her funeral service. At the height of her fame she received 300,000 letters a year and is recognized as the first business consultant astrologer in America.

aeromancy. °Divination from air and sky, from cloud shapes, °comets, spectral formations and other phenomena which in the past have caused speculation and consternation. Today some say that UFOs (unidentified flying objects), such as flying saucers, fall within this category. In the past aeromancy had a considerable vogue but today scepticism exists about its value and accuracy.

Agrippa. Heinrich Cornelius Agrippa von Nettesheim (1486–1535). His real name was Cornelis Heinrich, but he latinized it to Cornelius as was the fashion, and tacked on the bogus noble title of Agrippa von

4. Agrippa

Nettesheim. Talented and well read, he followed many vocations: alchemist, faith healer, demonologist, court astrologer, theologian, lawyer, doctor, historian, town orator, financial adviser, political agent and °occult scholar. He was an opportunist, working for Pope Leo X and for his rival, the Emperor Maximillian I, as occasion offered, switching sides to suit himself and as the fortunes of either vacillated. His best-known work is *De Occulta Philosophia* (Occult Philosophy), published in 3 volumes in 1531, which expounded the belief that Man is a miniature of God, made in His image and the universe (macrocosm) is built on a model of Man (microcosm) and consequently has a °soul. Everything in fact has a °soul and herbs, metals, stones, animals and natural phenomena have magical properties. He advanced a theory of °animal magnetism, and another that, as mules are sterile, a sure contraceptive for women was mule's urine. His wide-ranging mind enveloped the arts, sciences, music and astronomy; he dabbled in °necromancy and could conjure up the °spirits of the dead. His other great work is *De Incertitudine et Vanitate Scientiarum et Artium* (1529) (The Uncertainty and Vanity of the Sciences and the Arts). Though not as original a thinker as his great contemporary °Paracelsus, his erudition was profound and his knowledge encyclopedic; °ill. 4.

alchemy. The art of transmuting metals and other substances, the word being derived from the Arabic *al kimiya*, which means the magical craft of the Black Country or Northern Egypt, so-called from the contrast between the black soil of the Nile Delta and that of the South, which is sandy and reddish. There are four kinds of alchemy: **1.** Attempting to make gold from base metals with the aid of the °philosopher's stone; **2.** The search for an elixir that will preserve life indefinitely; **3.** The creation of life synthetically (without the aid of woman); **4.** A plane of thought. From the earliest times men have tried without success to convert base metals into gold. The Ancient Chinese believed that gold was imperishable and, if it could be diffused into microscopic particles and digested by the human body, it would provide old men with new teeth, eyes with keen sight and limbs with vitality. Scholars and eminent men wasted fortunes and ruined themselves trying to turn base metals into gold, and in 1317 Pope John XXII pronounced an edict against alchemy. Nicholas Flamel (1330–1418) is believed to have been an exception. For 2 florins he acquired a treatise on alchemy and, with the advice of a Jewish doctor he met in Spain, in 1382 he managed, with only his wife as witness, to convert half a pound of mercury into silver, and then into gold! With the proceeds from his experiments he gave lavishly to charity and endowed 14 hospitals, 3 chapels and 7 churches in Paris. His secret died with him.

alectryomancy. In Africa and among the °aborigines of Australia °divination from the actions of birds is practised. A black hen or game cock is used. Grain is sprinkled on the ground and, when the bird has finished pecking, the seer sees forms of prophetic significance in the patterns left. An alternative method is to recite the alphabet and note at which letter – if any – the cock crows, and a °prophecy is worked out based on this.

aleuromancy. Slips of paper on which

are written answers to questions are encased in balls of dough and baked. When cool, a ball is taken at random and cut open. The slip inside gives the answer sought. The American party game of 'fortune cookies' is a survival of this ancient ritual.

alomancy. The art of predicting events by sprinkling or throwing salt and interpreting the patterns made. This has given rise to the °superstition that spilling salt accidentally is unlucky.

American Society for Psychical Research. Founded in 1885 with Simon Newcomb, the astronomer, as president. Later it became a branch of the British °Society for Psychical Research and functioned in Boston under the guidance of °Hodgson until his death in 1905. A newly organized and independent ASPR was then established in New York with James H. Hyslop, former Professor of Logic and Ethics at Columbia University, as secretary and treasurer. Between 1906 and his death in 1920, Hyslop greatly expanded the scope of the Society's work and augmented its endowment fund. The *Journal* and *Proceedings*, which record a vast amount of scientific data, were started in 1917 and have continued to this day. The *Journal*, published quarterly, contains case reports, discussions, articles dealing with relevant trends and book reviews. *Proceedings*, issued from time to time, contains contributions too long for the *Journal*. The Society disseminates information by lectures, forums, seminars and workshops, and by counsel to researchers, students and others interested in its work. Among those closely associated with the ASPR were the physicists °Barrett, °Lodge and Lord Rayleigh, the physiologist °Richet, biologists Hans Driesch and Sir Alister Hardy, psychologists Gardner Murphy, °Thouless, °James and William McDougall, and philosophers H. Bergson, °Sidgwick, C.D. Broad, C.J. Ducasse and Price.

amulet. Anything worn to ward off evil, disease, °witchcraft, etc. In medieval times, it also meant medicines with magical properties; °charm; °talisman.

angel. A ministering spirit or divine messenger.

angelology. That part of theology which treats of °angels; doctrine as to °angels.

animal magnetism. When hypnotic phenomena were first observed, it was believed that a subtle fluid of magnetic nature passed from the operator to the subject; °hypnotism; °mesmerism.

animism. 1. The doctrine that the phenomena of animal life are produced by an immaterial *anima* or °soul, as distinct from matter. **2.** The attribution of living °souls to inanimate objects and natural phenomena. In extension °spiritualism is a belief that the °soul can exist without matter. Animism is a belief held by many primitive peoples that trees, earth, rocks and the elements possess supernatural powers.

anthroposophy. Knowledge of the nature of Man; wisdom. Anthroposophists form a flourishing cult founded by °Steiner. They investigate every kind of natural phenomenon to discover the cause of disease and search for true happiness; they investigate the influence of the planets on crops and animals, the mysteries of °astrology, and do research into cooking vessels and domestic fires, soil, astronomy, mathematics, economics, education, the arts, etc.

apantomancy. Forecasts made from the chance meeting with animals and birds, such as a black cat crossing one's path, which is said to bring good luck, or a raven, which is supposed to bring bad luck. Mexico City, for instance, was founded on a site where Aztecs observed an eagle flying from a cactus carrying a live snake – a most propitious sign. The scene is embodied in the city's coat-of-arms; °superstition.

apparitions. Immaterial appearances by real beings; °phantoms; °ghosts; °spectres.

apport. From French *apporter* (to bring). In spiritualism, it means motion or production of an object by a spiritualistic medium without apparent physical agency. Dr Nandor Fodor in his *Encyclopedia of Psychic Science* says: 'Arrival of various objects through an apparent penetration of matter.' Often dematerialization and rematerialization is thought to be part of the explanation of how this occurs. Some °mediums have produced apports out of the atmosphere. Bailey, for instance, used to pluck Roman coins out of the air. One moment his hands were empty, the next they were filled with *denarii*. The Public Museum in Launceston, Tasmania, has apports transported from the United States, and at Leland Stanford University Museum there are apports – fish, ancient earthen tablets, etc. – that Bailey plucked out of the air while in a sealed cage in Melbourne. A Mrs Maggs of Portsmouth, England, apported a vase from the tomb of an Ancient Syrian princess which she gave to °Leaf, who then presented it to °Conan Doyle; °asport; °teleportation.

Arundale, George Sydney, MA, LL.B, D.Litt. (1878–1945). He was educated in Italy and Germany, and graduated from Cambridge. Joined the °Theosophical Society in 1895 and was invited to India in 1903 by Dr Annie °Besant, where for 20 years he worked to promote Indian education, first as Professor of History and later as Principal of the Central

Ashmole

Hindu College, Benares (later Benares University), and then as Principal of the National University, Madras, and Minister of Education, Indore State. With Dr °Besant he was interned in 1917 for his involvement in the All India Home Rule League. He travelled and lectured extensively in Europe, India and Australia and was at different periods General Secretary of the °Theosophical Society in England, Australia and India. In 1920 he married Shrimati Rukmina Devi, a Brahmin girl who came from a theosophic family. She made Hindu classical dancing, which had become degraded in India, her profession and showed that disciplined dancing and posturing were repetitions of cosmic rhythms set in motion by the Creator. In this way her dancing interpreted divine events, increased perception and brought °ecstasy. In 1934 Arundale was elected President of the °Theosophical Society, succeeding Dr °Besant. He made substantial contributions to theosophical literature, with *Nirvana, Kundalini,* and *The Lotus Fire.* He died in Adyar; °ill. 5.

5. Dr George Arundale

Ashmole, Elias (1617–1692). Son of a saddler, but of good family, he became a solicitor and Lord of the Manor of Bradfield, Berks. He was a close friend of William °Lilly and through him of the astrologer John Booker. While a certain William Backhouse lay dying he gave Ashmole the secret of the °philosopher's stone. John °Dee left Ashmole his books and manuscripts, and the latter grew in wealth and influence till Charles II appointed him Windsor Herald. John Tradescant, Keeper of the Botanic Gardens in Chelsea, left Ashmole his collection of curiosities from all parts of the world, which filled 12 wagons, and this, together with his own extensive library, he bequeathed to Oxford University, where it forms the nucleus of the world-famous Ashmolean Museum. His interest in °astrology, at which he became an expert, was whetted by a manuscript sent to him by the mathematician–astrologer John Blagrave of Reading.

asports. The reverse of °apports; the disappearance of objects from the seance room through barriers of intervening matter and their appearance in another place. In the Millesimo seances, for example, the Marquis Centurione Scotto and Mme Fabrair Rossi, members of the circle, were tapped by a little parchment drum, and Mme Rossi and Mme la Marquise Luisa felt their hands squeezed by 2 iron mittens. At the end of the °seance these objects were no longer in the room. The drum was found in the large salon, where previously it had stood, while the mittens were found at the foot of the suit of armour from which they had been detached.

Astaroth. Being credited with power in °black °magic; °Beelzebub.

astral body. Enveloping the material body is an ethereal substance with a very high rate of °vibration, neither matter nor mere force, and more tenacious than any substance yet discovered. °Yogis called it *akasha*. When in a state of *samadhi* (in which the mind becomes identified with the object of °meditation) the °soul is liberated from *brahma-randhra* (head fontanelle), which starts to function through the astral body, even in points of space remote from the astral body. When this has been achieved, the °yogi withdraws his °soul from the astral body to the physical body along a fine filament of ethereal substance which connects the two. Should this filament be severed the °soul in the astral body cannot return and the body perishes. The astral body is subject neither to cold nor heat, nor to any other physical conditions. Astral beings can see, hear, smell, feel and taste; they have 3 eyes: 2 partly closed and the °third (or astral) eye, placed vertically in the forehead, open. Astral beings can regenerate their bodies by lifetronic force or mantric vibrations, and communication between astral inhabitants is carried on by °telepathy or television; °ether; °mantra; °ill. 6.

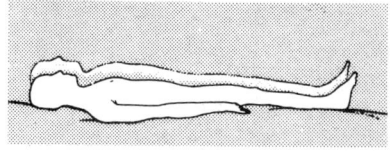

6. Astral body

astral projection. In this the °astral body leaves the material body. There is evidence from the earliest times of astral projection. William Blake swore he watched his brother's °astral body leave his material body at the moment of death. In 1877 °Gurney, °Myers and Podmore published *Phantasms of the Living* in which 700 authenticated cases of

astrology

this phenomenon were given. William Gerhardi, the novelist, wrote of his own experiences. In the 1960s Charles T. Tart, Assistant Professor of Psychology at the University of California, carried out controlled experiments, an account of which appeared in the journal of the New York Parapsychology Foundation. In 1966 Dr Charles McCreery of the Oxford Institute of Psychological Research appealed to the public for first-hand accounts of 'out-of-body' experiences and, of 300 undergraduates questioned at Oxford, 12 claimed to have left their bodies at some time. Apart from °yogis there are a few who can leave their bodies at will but most people have no control over the °astral body. J. B. S. Haldane, the famous scientist, described how he saw himself sitting in his favourite armchair smoking a pipe. 'Irregular' was his word for the phenomenon; 'indigestion' is how he explained it.

astrology. Derived from the Greek *astron* (star) and *logos* (discourse). In Old French and Middle English *astronomie* was the earlier and more general word, *astrologie* coming in later for the art or practice of applying astronomy to the °prediction of events, natural and moral. The purpose of astrology is to predict, not to prophesy. Predict is derived from the Latin *prae* (before) and *dicere* (to say) and it means 'to foretell'. Astrological °predictions about political events, trends in science, education, art, the money markets, the weather and even sporting contests, may be deduced from known facts. Predictions are reached by logical reasoning and judgement. The astrologer works from a firm basis: time, date, year and place of birth. He does not need °intuition, °second sight or °clairvoyance any more than a physician does. A °prophecy is entirely different. It is the declaration of a prophet and the word comes from the Latin *propheta* or one who speaks and interprets the will of God. Prophecies are not based on facts or reasoning but on inspired revelations. The astrologer predicts events from the positions of the planets at the moment of birth. He makes a chart consisting of 12 houses and the positions of the planets in those houses; their subsequent movements are printed in an ephemeris for that year. This enables him to judge the character of the subject, his tendency to disease and milestones in his life. Indications given in the chart are analogous to the symptoms by which a physician diagnoses and prescribes. In astrology these facts, and in medicine symptoms, are the basis on which practitioners diagnose or predict, and success depends on knowledge, skill and experience. Thus a number of astrologers primed with the same facts, or physicians with the same symptoms, may arrive

astrology

at somewhat different but basically the same conclusions. No one knows when astrology originated or where the art was first practised. In Mesopotamia, Egypt, Babylon, Assyria and Chaldea the stars were regarded as the source and, at the same time, the heralds of all events, and priests studied the art of astrology. In India astrology and worship were linked with the stars, and to this day Brahmins are considered the finest exponents of astrology. In Ancient Greece it permeated the entire concept of nature and played an important part in religious worship; in Rome it ruled both public and private life for 500 years. With the spread of Christianity, however, it lost its commanding position and in AD 321 Constantine issued an edict threatening magicians and astrologers with death. St Augustine (AD 345–430) condemned astrology and it disappeared from Western Europe for several centuries. But astrology survived in Jewish literature and the *Sefer Zohar* and *Sefer Yezirah*, written after the *Talmud*, are full of rules dealing with astrological calculations and interpretations. The Arabs, always interested in the subject, revived astrology and Caliph Al-Mansur, founder of Baghdad, encouraged scholars to study astronomy. In AD 777 Jacob ben Tarik founded the Baghdad School of Astronomy and Astrology. When, during the Crusades (1096–1228), Arabic learning spread to Spain, France and even to Oxford, Hebrew scholars regarded astrology as a necessary part of their talmudic and cabalistic studies. Popes and emperors became devotees of astrology: Charles IV, Charles V, Popes Sextus IV, Julius II, Leo X, Clement VI and Paul III. The famous theologian and astrologer Pierre d'Ailly (1350–1420) inspired Columbus to make his famous voyage. The Medicis were zealous patrons of astrology and it was popularized in France by Catherine de Medici, whose court astrologer was °Nostradamus. Astrology blossomed simultaneously in China, India, Egypt and Central America more than 40 centuries ago among peoples living thousands of miles from each other, separated by seas, deserts and mountains. According to the *History of Chinese Astronomy* by A.J. Pearce it was widely established by 1752 BC and Richard R. Allen in *A Manual of Cheirosophy* says it was in 2637 BC. In India, where history has for centuries been handed down by word of mouth, °horoscopes were drawn up in 3102 BC. In *Study of Two Americas*, Stuart Chase says that the high priests of the Mayas observed the heavens 4,000 years ago and the Maya calendar was able to distinguish without duplication any given day in 370,000 years. °Gipsies, who are thought to have originated in India, have practised a form of astrology

augury

since the dawn of civilization; it has always flourished in India where, if they can afford it, parents have the °horoscopes of their children cast so that they may take advantage of lucky periods, guard against misfortune and marry suitable partners. In the USA there are more than 25,000 registered °seers (not all astrologers), some 200 newspapers print daily °horoscopes, and *The Moon Sign Book* has a circulation of more than a million, which increases yearly. In France interest in astrology is nationwide. *Horoscope*, a monthly magazine, has a readership of 400,000 and *Ici Paris* gets 200–300 letters each week on the subject. Despite the fact that °fortune-telling is proscribed by the Church, France has 500,000 practising astrologers, palmists and clairvoyants who between them receive half a million pounds a week from clients. The magazine *Elle*, which runs a feature by the Italian astrologer Francesco Waldner, has a circulation of 750,000 but the proprietors claim that it is read by 58 per cent of the population because each copy is passed from hand to hand. In Britain, where astrology was popularized by R. H. °Naylor, those who read the tabloids and the more sensational papers often turn first to the astrological column, many successful businessmen employ astrological consultants and even Members of Parliament and men high in the professions turn to astrologers for advice. Dr Carl °Jung, founder of analytical psychology, had the courage to confess his faith in astrology. In a message to the Indian *Astrological Magazine* he said: 'I can tell you that I've been interested in this particular activity of the human mind for more than 30 years. As I am a psychologist, I'm chiefly interested in the particular light the horoscope sheds on certain complications in the character. In cases of difficult psychological diagnosis I usually get a horoscope in order to have a further point of view from an entirely different angle. I must say that I have very often found that the astrological data elucidated certain points which I otherwise would not have been able to understand.' A number of well-known medical men also use astrology to help them in making diagnoses.

augury. The arts of °divination, comprising all forms of °prophecy, though chiefly interpretations of the future based on signs and °omens.

aura, human. An emanation of one or more of the 7 principles of Man, projecting from several inches up to 2 or 3 feet beyond the body and visible only to those with a highly developed °psychic power, though a few with 'inferior sight' can see grosser manifestations of part of the aura. Auras, which are body radiations, vary in °colour, depending on

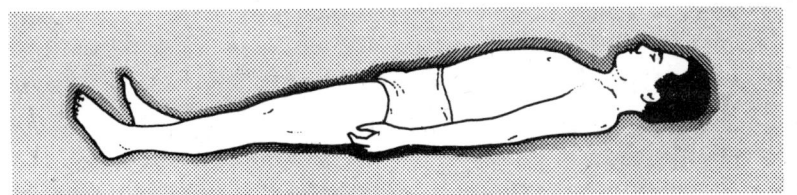

7. Human aura

the nature, character and state of health of the subject, and change as health or mental attitudes change. The aura of a saint, a rich blue-violet, represents the acme of religious feeling. The grossest form of aura is the health aura which extends a distance of 2 or 3 feet from the body, is oval and sometimes is referred to as the 'auric egg'. It is either colourless or bluish-white and streaked with fine lines which extend outwards from the body like stiff bristles. When vitality is impaired the 'bristles' droop or are tangled, twisted or curled. Auras are of different colours, each with its own characteristics. Steely grey represents selfishness; dull grey, fear and horror; dark grey, depression and melancholy; green, jealousy, and if generated by anger, will be flecked with bright red; slate-green, low deceit; emerald, tolerance, an easy-going nature, adaptability, courtesy and worldly wisdom; dull red, a sensual animal nature; flashing red, anger, and, if imposed on a black background, malice and hatred, but, if on a green background, jealousy mingled with anger; crimson, love; dull crimson, gross and sensual; bright crimson, a higher feeling; rose tinted, a high form of love; reddish-brown, avarice and greed; orange, pride and ambition; yellow (all shades), intellectual power; mustard, a lower intelligence; as the yellow grows lighter intelligence increases and gold means great intellect and reasoning power; blue, religious thought; feeling and emotion are indicated by shades varying from indigo to rich violet; light blue represents spirituality. The finest human beings have auras that sparkle and twinkle like the stars; Walter J. °Kilner; °ill. 7.

Aurobindo, Sri (1872–1950). The name by which Aurobindo Ghose, one of the most famous of modern °yogis, is known. Born of wealthy parents in Bengal, he was educated at Manchester Grammar School and King's College, Cambridge, where he headed the list in the Indian Civil Service examination but was rejected because he could not ride. On his return to India he took service with the Maharaja Sayajji

automatic writing

Rao Gaekwar of Baroda, but his mind was too active for service in an Indian state and he was soon embroiled in nationalist agitation. He edited *Yogantar* and *Karma Yogin*, inspired a school of activism and was arrested and thrown into prison, where his spiritual transformation took place. When set free, he retired to Pondicherry to study, meditate and practise °yoga, and founded the magazine *Arya*, in which he published his *Essays On The Gita*. Hindus, Muslims and Christians, among them Sir Akbar Hydari and Miss Slade, daughter of an English admiral, came under his influence. His last years were spent in silence and seclusion, giving a *darshan* (opportunity for followers to see him) twice a year, for, in accordance with yoga thought, he believed that physical contact is unnecessary and guidance can be given over any distance. The subjects of his writings ranged from °yoga and philosophy to art, education and the Renaissance of India. When Aurobindo died, the Chief Medical Officer in French India certified that his body remained fresh for 2 days (in a climate where decomposition sets in within 12 hours) and was pervaded by an °aura of light.

automatic writing. Method of communication with the unseen world. The subject takes a pen or pencil, places a sheet of paper in front of him and his hand is moved by some power over which he has no control. Some automatic writing makes sense; other kinds result in gibberish, and books are said to have been written under outside influence. The Rev. Vale Owen, for instance, wrote at an average speed of 24 words a minute on 4 evenings each week for months at a stretch, some of his work being dictated by his mother who had passed over, and the rest by an entity named Zabdiel. Between 1901 and 1930 the °Society for Psychical Research examined more than 3,000 scripts produced either by automatic writing, or under °trance, in dead languages or languages unknown to the writer. Inspirational fiction has often been produced in this way.

automatism. Organic functions, or inhibitions, not controlled by the °conscious self.

automatist. A writing °medium; one who is able to actuate a °ouija board or does °automatic writing; °automatism. Geraldine °Cummins, Hester °Dowden and Rosemary Brown are well-known automatists.

auto-suggestion. Suggestion arising from the individual himself; Emile °Coué.

avatara. A rare being, neither reincarnated nor in the process of evolution, who descends from the divine regions into human form. Avataras appear at periods in world history when the cyclic course of events needs a change which can be effected only by them. Confucius, Christ, Buddha, Bodidharma, Lao Tzu and °Mahomet are said to be avataras; sometimes Ramakrishna, Wesley, Knox, Calvin and Luther are also cited as examples.

B

Bach, Edward, MB, BS, MRCS (1886–1936). Graduate of University College Hospital, who, after practising in Harley Street, discarded allopathy for homeopathy and was appointed bacteriologist and pathologist to the London Homeopathic Hospital. He was highly psychic and eventually established his own system of healing by extracting essences from the petals of flowers. He said that earth, air and water nurtured the plant and the sun gave it power and imparted beneficial healing °vibrations to its flowers. By placing his hands over the petals Bach was able to say whether it had healing properties, and name the diseases it overcame. By floating the petals in a bowl of spring water while the dew was still on them and exposing them to the sun he extracted tinctures which, preserved in brandy, enabled him to cure many diseases which originate in the mind and afflict the body. The medical discoveries of Dr Bach (pronounced to rhyme with batch) have been put into practice and used by physicians all the world over; °floromancy.

Bael. Being credited with power in °black °magic; °Beelzebub.

Bagnall, Oscar. Author of *The Origin and Properties of the Human Aura* (1937); °aura; °Kilner.

Bahá 'í Faith. Was founded by Bahá 'u 'lláh; Abdul-Bahá was its prime exemplar. Bahá 'u 'lláh's real name was Mirza Husayan Ali and his adopted name means 'Glory of God'. He was born in Tehran, Persia, in 1817 and was the son of a Vazir (Minister of State). At the age of 25, in response to divine command, he rejected high office in the state and preached a new religion, for which he was persecuted. He taught continuous revelation, the unity of all classes, races, peoples and religions, the Unity of God and his prophets, and the unity of all creation. His followers believe him to be the prom-

Balfour, Arthur J. (1848–1930). One of the early members of the °Society for Psychical Research and a member of the Council in 1887, which included 8 FRSs and 2 bishops. He was educated at Eton and Cambridge, entered Parliament in 1874 and was successively Chief Secretary for Ireland, First Lord of the Treasury, and Prime Minister, succeeding Lord Salisbury. Among his publications were *A Defence of Philosophic Doubt, The Foundations of Belief* and his Gifford Lectures under the title *Theism and Humanism*.

banshee. Female °elf. A supernatural being who appears in homes in the Highlands of Scotland and in Ireland, and wails when an inmate is about to die.

Barbanell, Maurice. Founded *Psychic News* in 1932 and, with Hannen °Swaffer, made many experiments with °mediums.

Barrett, Prof. Sir W. F. (1884–1925). Distinguished Dublin physicist and a founder member of the °Society for Psychical Research (SPR). In 1881 Edmund Dawson Rogers, a journalist and spiritualist, was visited by Barrett. They discussed °psychic matters and Rogers suggested that a society should be started to attract 'some of the best minds which had hitherto held aloof from the pursuit of the inquiry'. Men of Barrett's reputation gave the °SPR a standing it would not otherwise have had. Barrett ultimately became a Presi-

8. Abdul-Bahá, the prime exponent of the Bahá'í Faith

ised one of all faiths who is to unite the whole world in the love of God. The movement has no clergy or ritual and members are united as a single family. °Healing by touch and by contact with a healthy body, so that power from the stronger passes to the weaker, hydrotherapy and vegetarianism were all originally advocated, though are now infrequently practised. Their literature is translated into 450 languages and dialects, and is established in 140 independent countries. There are 56,000 Bahá'í centres throughout the world, of which 500 are in Britain. Tolstoy called it 'the highest and purest religion'; °ill. 8.

9. Sir W. F. Barrett

dent of the Society; °American SPR; °ill. 9.

Bashir, Mir (1907–). A Kashmiri, resident in Britain since 1948 and one of the leading exponents of °palmistry in the world. Though he predicts with astonishing accuracy, his role is mainly that of adviser: to men and women on the professions they and their children are fitted for; on marriage; on character and tendencies to crime; on business; on diseases that show in the palm long before the symptoms are apparent to physicians. He has collaborated with physicians and crime experts, and his library of hand prints, which exceeds 50,000, must be the largest of its kind. Author of *How to Read Hands* and *The Art of Hand Analysis*; °ill. 10.

Bastet. Cat-headed goddess of fertility in Egypt; °cat.

10. Mir Bashir

Beelzebub (Bael-Zeebub). Mentioned as God of Ekron (2 Kings 1:2). The Canaanites worshipped in his temple, which was never polluted by flies, which in the East are considered unclean insects. Beelzebub is mentioned in Matthew 12:27 and

Behemoth

again in Luke 11:15: 'But some of them said He casteth out devils through Beelzebub, chief of the devils'. In °black °magic he is credited with immense power along with °Belial, °Bael, °Forcas, °Buer, °Marchocias, °Astaroth and °Behemoth.

Behemoth. Being credited in °black °magic with having power; °Beelzebub.

Belial. Being credited in °black °magic with having power; °Beelzebub.

Bender, Prof. Hans (1907–   ). Born in Freiburg-im-Breisgau, Germany. PH.D. Bonn University, 1933; MD, Strasbourg University, 1941. Director of Institut für Granzgebiete der Psychologie und Psychohygiene, Freiburg from 1950. Held various academic appointments before becoming Director of the Institut, where he has become world-famous for his investigations into °psychic phenomena.

Benham, W. G. Born late 19th century. Author of *The Laws of Scientific Palm Reading* (1900), a standard work on the subject; °palmistry.

Besant, Dr Annie (1847–1933). An Irish girl born in London, who married the Rev. Frank Besant, brother of Sir Walter Besant. She worked with Charles Bradlaugh and embraced Socialism. Her life changed dramatically when George Bernard Shaw sent her a copy of *The Secret Doctrine* by Helena °Blavatsky for review. After skimming through both volumes, she rushed out to find the author and threw herself bodily at her feet. Annie Besant claimed to have been 'born' twice. At her second 'birth' she discovered °theosophy. Her third 'birth' occurred when she visited India, where she founded the Hindu College in Benares, and succeeded Colonel °Olcott as President of the °Theosophical Society in 1907, an office which she held till her death. She established the All India Home Rule League and was interned for anti-British political activities. In India she is regarded as an °avatara and a saint; °ill. 11.

11. Dr Annie Besant

Besson, Pierre. Born 20th century. A believer in the °occult, a practitioner of °magic and a well-known dowser.

Took a course at the International School of °Radiesthesia in Niće and then invented his own apparatus for diagnosing diseases from saliva, for which he prescribes cures. In order to test him, people sometimes send him sheets of blotting paper stained with other liquids but his equipment invariably fails to find any trace of disease. Doctors, who admit they are baffled, send him the saliva of patients, which he diagnoses accurately. Has published, in collaboration with M.A. Delobel, *A System of Practical Radiesthesia*; °dowsing.

bilocation. The ability to be in two places, often far apart, at the same time. The best-known example is that of Alphonsus Liguori, a prominent Neapolitan, who was seen on the same day and at the same hour in places 4 days travelling distance apart on 21 September 1744. St Francis Xavier was also seen by sailors in a boat on the China Seas when he was in fact on board a ship captained by Duarte de Gama, thousands of miles away. There are many other recorded cases.

birth stone. All objects, living and inanimate, exude °vibrations. According to °astrology the radiations produced by some gems beneficially affect people born under one °sign more than another and it is generally accepted that the correct birthstones are: Aries, diamond; Taurus, emerald; Gemini, agate; Cancer, ruby; Leo, sardonyx; Virgo, sapphire; Libra, opal; Scorpio, topaz; Sagittarius, turquoise; Capricorn, garnet; Aquarius, amethyst; Pisces, bloodstone; °gem.

black magic. °Magic involving the invocation of devils. A branch of witchcraft better avoided by serious students of the occult. As the aim of black magic is to harm, injure, or kill, its practice is illegal in many countries.

black mass. Originated in France during the 16th century by Catherine de Medici (1519–1589), who was said to be responsible for the Massacre of St Bartholomew. The mass takes a variety of forms, most of them at an altar on which stands a crucifix, which, together with the host, is desecrated and befouled; animals and birds are killed, the communicants stained with blood, and the Devil invoked.

Blavatsky, Helena Patrovna (1831–1891). Known as HPB to her followers, she was born in Etakernoslav, Russia, the daughter of Col. Peter Haln de Rottenstein-Hahu, nobleman, and granddaughter of Princess Dolgorouki. She was co-founder, with Colonel °Olcott, of the °Theosophical Society of New York. As a child she was clairvoyant and clairaudiant, and talked with *roussalkas* (wood °nymphs) and *domovoys* (°nature spirits). She travelled in China, India, Africa, Tibet and South America, possessed

bones, throwing

°occult powers and was in direct communication with the mahatmas Koot Moomi and Moorya, who lived in Tibet. She practised and wrote books on °yoga and the °occult, and made 100,000 converts in America and India. The °Society for Psychical Research sent out 2 members to investigate her, who later turned out to be self-confessed perjurers. They labelled her a fraud, but °Besant and °Leadbeater thought otherwise. Her best-known works were *Isis Unveiled* and *The Secret Doctrine*. She died in India; °ill. 12.

12. Helena Blavatsky

bones, throwing. A method used by °ju-ju men and *inyangas* (°witch doctors) to look into the minds of others, to see into the future, to learn what is happening at a distance, and to see where lost property lies or where stolen property has been hidden. In Africa the practice is called *shaya matembo*. The *inyanga* takes a handful of small animal or snake bones in his hands, rattles them like dice and throws them in front of his client. He then concentrates his thoughts on them and pictures, events, places, words and even thoughts take shape, and after a period of contemplation his conclusions are delivered. One theory is that the *inyanga* hypnotizes himself and is able to project his mind into space and reveal the information sought. °Witch doctors do not merely discover and reveal – they also advise and cure.

Book of Fate. After the Nile Campaign of 1799, French Egyptologists conveyed an enormous amount of loot to Napoleon, which is now housed in the museums of France. One item was a volume, now known as Napoleon's *Book of Fate*, which contains the key to °divination written in hieroglyphics on papyrus. With Egyptian help this was translated and the book was found in Napoleon's carriage after Waterloo. The papyrus disintegrated but copies were made. It contains 32 symbols (10 more were added by Kirchenhoffer), some of which, such as the °sun, the °moon, death and the shattered tower, figure in the °tarot.

Book of the Dead. The most arcane

treatise on cosmogony and psychology apart from the *Upanishads* and the *Puranas* of the Hindus. It was found by Lepsius who called it 'Das Todenbuch'. It defied translation for many years, but eventually Jean François Champollion and his brother, with the aid of the Rosetta Stone which gave the key to the hieroglyphics, made sense of it. The Egyptian name means 'Book of The Master of The Secret House', and its texts are inscribed on the descending passages of the Pyramid of Unas, built during the 5th and 6th dynasties, *c.* 4000 BC. The book is a scripture of life which reveals the finer world, the higher powers of Man and the way in which he can travel the road to immortality.

Borley Rectory. A large Victorian parsonage built in 1863 on the foundations of an ancient monastery by the Rev. Henry Bull, squire–parson, who was °psychic. In 1875–1876 he added a wing and in 1892 his son, the Rev. Harry Bull, who was also interested in the °occult, succeeded him and lived there till 1927. From the time it was built °apparitions were seen and strange noises heard. In 1928 the Rev. Eric Smith became the incumbent and, experiencing uncanny phenomena, he got in touch with the *Daily Mirror*, who sent first a reporter and then °Price to investigate. °Price lived there for some time, then in 1937 he rented the place for a year and wrote 2 bestsellers, *The Most Haunted House in England* and *The End of Borley Rectory*. Prof. C. E. M. Joad, who stayed a night there with °Price, swore that a °poltergeist threw a cake of soap which hit him in the eye. In 1939 the rectory, which was uninhabited, was destroyed by a mysterious fire and in 1956 Dr E. J. Dingwall, the Cambridge scientist, wrote *The Haunting of Borley Rectory*, in which he refuted the idea that it was ever haunted. No one has been able, however, to account for the thumpings, rattlings, sounds of footsteps, patches of green and blue iridescence, powerful cooking odours and waves of perfume that pervaded the place and continued after the publication of Dingwall's book. In 1959 the land was cleared and used for growing mushrooms, but Mr Williams, a retired engineer who lived in the adjoining cottage, experienced similar phenomena, and in 1963 Montague Elelman, who took a piece of building fabric from Borley, described on the radio the unnerving happenings he had experienced, which scientific investigators have not been able to explain.

Bozzano, Prof. Ernest (1862–1945). Italian psychologist considered by many to be the greatest authority on °psychic research and his *Animis and Spiritualism* the ablest working hypothesis of the survival of the body after death. His researches into the °materialization and dematerialization of the °phantom Nepenthes satisfied the most stringent critics. She materialized and dematerialized under the control of Mme d'Esperance, she was photographed, gave a paraffin mould of her hand and wrote a message in Ancient Greek (a language unknown to the audience) declaring she had lived in Greece. Another of his materializing °mediums was Eusapia °Palladino.

Brahan Seer (Kenneth Mackenzie). Born at the beginning of the 17th century, he was noted for many prophecies that came to pass; others are as yet unfulfilled, though some of the most unlikely may still come true. One which seemed ridiculous when he made it is now within the bounds of possibility: he said, 'However unlikely it may now appear, the Island of Lewis will be laid waste by a destructive war.' He also predicted the doom of the Seaforth family, which came to pass not long after his death.

Brown, Rosemary. A widow living in Balham, London, who is °psychic and says she is in touch with Liszt, Chopin, Debussy, Brahms and Beethoven, who enable her to produce compositions in their genre. Musicians are baffled, for though it is possible to produce one or two pieces similar to those of the great masters, to create complete works in their style would seem impossible.

buddhi. Wisdom, which should not be confused with either knowledge or learning. A realization of Man's affinity with all living creatures. Only when Man is conscious of other forms of life and treats them with friendliness, understanding and compassion is it possible for him to achieve buddhi; °karma; °mantra; °soul.

Buddhism (the Middle Way). The inspirational teachings of Siddhartha Gotama (born 560 BC). Founded (c. 535 BC) on the 4 pillars or truths: 1. all individual (selfish) existence is misery; 2. individuals are attached to worldly things, which are ephemeral; 3. true happiness can be found in detachment from the material things; 4. °nirvana can be reached by following the 'eightfold path'. Buddhism has no god and no commandments, merely 5 precepts which disciples must follow to the best of their ability. If they do not succeed, all will not be lost; they should do the best they can. The precepts are: 1. do not kill, though sometimes one has to for the sake of others; 2. do not steal the money, goods, wife or character of another; 3. avoid wrongful sexual acts, e.g. adultery, rape, or seduction for profit; 4. do not lie except to avoid hurting the feelings of another and provided that no one is harmed; 5. avoid all forms of intoxicants which lead to temptation: drink, drugs or bribes.

Buer. In °black °magic a being who is credited with power; °Beelzebub.

C

Cabala. °Kabalah.

Cagliostro, Count Alessandro (1743–1795). His real name was Giuseppe Balsamo. He was born in Malta, orphaned in early childhood and befriended by Althotas. A °psychic, he lived for some time in Medina. He travelled to Mecca and Egypt where he was recognized as a 'superior'. He was received into the Order of the Knights of Malta. The most famous °medium of his day, he could diagnose and cure disease, mesmerize and tell the future. He travelled to London in 1776, where he made several astonishing °predictions, then to Russia and Poland where he cured hundreds of 'incurables', founded an Occult Lodge and transmuted lead into gold. The Holy Office ordered his arrest in 1789 and he died a prisoner in the Castle of San Leo, where he was buried in an unconsecrated grave on the highest point of the rock; °alchemy; °mesmerism.

Canon, Dr Alexander, PH.D, FRCS, MD. Psychiatrist and research scientist at Colney Hatch Mental Hospital in Britain. He investigated various aspects of the °occult, practised °yoga and travelled in India and Tibet. In his book *Invisible Influence* he stated that he had met the Great Ones and that once he, his porters and their luggage were levitated over a chasm. Because of this claim he was dismissed by the London County Council, but brought an action against them and was reinstated. Not long after he retired, he set up in Harley Street and employed 2 °mediums to help him in diagnosis. In 1939 he moved to the Isle of Man, where he started a nursing home called The Isle of Man Clinic For Nervous Diseases. He died during the Second World War.

cargo cult. Started in New Guinea in 1919 when a man named Evara fell into a °trance while hunting, turned up in his village unharmed 4 days later, said that a sorcerer had entered his stomach, then went into convulsions, during which he revealed that a flying machine filled with gifts from their ancestors would soon arrive. He continued to prophesy. Papuans in other villages started having convulsions and the cult spread. Evara claimed to be divine and promised a millennium. Airstrips were cut in the jungle and, when a Curtiss flying-boat arrived in 1922 bearing gifts for the people, their beliefs were confirmed. The cult was almost destroyed by the contact with white men, though in remote areas many Papuans still believe that planes bearing gifts will arrive again to make them rich and happy.

Carrel, Dr Alexis (1873–1944). Born near Lyons, France, and died in Paris. After qualifying and teaching in Lyons, he went to America in 1905 to join the Rockefeller Institute of Medical Research. He received the Nobel Prize for medicine in 1912 and served as a surgeon in the 1914 war. In 1939 he returned to France from the USA and worked on a mechanical heart. Wrote many scientific works, but his best known is the popular *Man, The Unknown*. He believed in the °occult, °spirit healing and healing by hands, and testified that some of the cures at Lourdes could only have been achieved by °faith. He experimented with °hypnosis, °telepathy and °vibrations.

Carroll-Clark, E. H., LDS, RCS (Eng). (1905–   ). South African by nationality, he was a graduate of the London Hospital and practised in London for 40 years. He was a pioneer in the practice of °hypnosis in dentistry and author of *How You Can Save Your Children's Teeth*.

cartomancy. Predicting the future with cards; °prediction; °tarot; °zenner.

cartopedy. Predicting the future and assessing character and ability by examining the lines on the soles of the feet. An ancient art which originated in Persia and was later taken to India by the Moghuls. The royal cartopedist was always consulted when a bride was chosen for the emperor.

cat. Has always been associated with the °occult. In Ancient Egypt it was sacrilege to kill one and when a cat died it was buried with full funeral rites. °Bastet was the cat-headed goddess of fertility and maternity. In Ancient Rome Tiberius Gracchus so admired the cat's independence that he put an image of it in the Temple of Liberty as freedom's best friend. All over Europe in the Middle Ages black cats were regarded as incarnations of the °Devil. °Witches always kept black cats and the Devil's favourite disguise was said to be a black cat, despite which they are considered to bring luck. Charles I had a black cat and a superstitious dread of losing it. When eventually it fell ill and died, he exclaimed: 'My luck has gone!' Next day he was arrested; °ill. 13.

Cayce, Edgar (1877–1945). One of the most remarkable clairvoyants and spiritual healers of modern times. Born in Kentucky, USA, his powers became evident when he 'saw' and held conversations with his grand-

13. Bronze cat from the Roman Period (?), after 30 BC (*British Museum. Crown Copyright*)

father, who had been thrown from a horse and killed. At school he could not concentrate till one day a voice said, 'Sleep and give us a chance to help you.' He slept with a book under his pillow and on waking could repeat every word of it from memory. At school a baseball accident injured his spine and destroyed the balance of his mind, but he diagnosed the trouble and told his parents to make poultices from herbs. These were applied to the base of his skull and cured him. He in turn cured thousands whom doctors had labelled incurable by going into °trances, diagnosing their ailments and prescribing remedies. Cayce died from overwork and, after his death, the Association for Research and Enlightenment, Virginia, was formed on the basis of the 14 million words he had written on 10,000 subjects; °clairvoyance.

Celts. °Kelts.

chakras, the six. Nerve centres of power as taught in hatha-yoga: 1. at the base of the spine; 2. at the level of the genital organs; 3. in the area of the navel; 4. around the heart; 5. in the throat; 6. in the forehead. Major B. D. Basu, IMS (Prize Essay, *Guy's Hospital Gazette*, 1899) says that these chakras approximate to: 1. sacral plexus; 2. prostatic; 3. epigastric; 4. cardiac; 5. pharyngeal; 6. cavernous. When one has advanced sufficiently to awaken *kundalini*, the vital force flows through the interior of the spinal cord, awakens the chakras and sensitizes them so that °psychic powers are attained; °ill. 14.

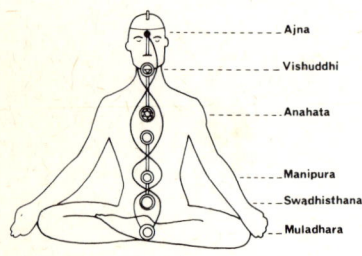

14. The six chakras

Chapman, George. Born early 20th century. °Spirit healer and °psychic surgeon, from Aylesbury, England, who practises distant healing, the laying-on of hands and °psychic surgery through the °medium of William Lang, FRCS, of the London Hospital, who founded the Ophthalmological Society in 1881. *Healing By Hands* by J. Bernard Hutton, on whom Chapman operated successfully for near-blindness, gives an account of his work.

Charcot, Jean Martin (1825–1893). Born in Paris. Appointed Medical Attendant at the Salipêtrière, an institution for insane and afflicted women, where he was the first physician to cure mental disorders by °hypnosis. Charcot's Disease consists of a change in the joints during *locomotor ataxia.*

charm. Object, often made of stone, worn to avert evil or to bring luck; a spell. Plato was one of the first to contribute to the idea that inanimate objects produce °vibrations which can affect humans. He maintained that gems owe their origin to the stars. The tiny figure of the Japanese god Ho-tei is supposed to bring good luck; the Cornish believe that Joan-the-Wad, a pisky charm, protects its wearers. As the theory can be neither substantiated nor disproved, millions of people wear charms 'just in case'; °birthstone; °gems.

Cheiro (Count Louis Hamon) (1866–1939). Descendant of a Huguenot family that settled in Ireland, he studied philosophy and poetry and became immersed in the °occult. He travelled in India where he was taught *hastirika* (science of the lines of the hand), and later he learned °astrology in the Vatican library. He told Charles Russell the exact day he would be appointed Lord Chief Justice of England, King Edward VII and Lord Kitchener when they would die, Parnell that he would face political ruin, Mark Twain, then on the verge of bankruptcy, that his fortunes would revive and he would be rich again, and, 10 years before the event, he predicted the abdication of Edward VIII. He died in California at the exact time and place he had predicted. He wrote a number of works on °palmistry and °prediction, including *Cheiro's World Predictions, Confessions of a Modern Seer, Language of The Hand* and *Cheiro's Book of Numbers*; °ill. 15.

15. Cheiro (Count Louis Hamon)

chirognomy. °Prediction from the shape of the hand; °palmistry.

Christian Science. Religion founded by Mary Baker °Eddy. Has followers in every continent and some 350 churches in Britain. There are altogether 500,000 members and each branch maintains a library and a reading room. The religion is a conventional Protestant one. Members neither smoke nor drink. Drugs are taboo and so is discussion of physical ailments because 'sick thoughts make sick bodies'. Converts are required to rise each morning and study the lesson-sermon for the day. They must give up gambling and profanity. All disease, they say, is caused by the mind and is usually the product of fear. It is permissible, however, to summon medical help for broken bones or contagious diseases, and decayed teeth may be extracted; otherwise, the mind cures all. Some astonishing cures have been recorded, including diseases such as cancer. The central authority, the Mother Church in Boston, USA, has a board of directors who administer the organization, but each branch is independent. It is the only Christian Church in which complete equality of the sexes is observed.

clairaudience. Derived from the Latin *clarus* (clear) and *audire* (hear); the gift possessed by °mediums and other sensitives of hearing the voices of those who have passed over.

clairvoyance. Derived from the Latin *clarus* (clear) and *videre* (see); the gift possessed by °mediums and other sensitives of seeing the forms of those who have passed over, and hearing their voices. Clairvoyants pass messages from the departed to the living, but no genuine clairvoyant will claim to be 100 per cent correct for, if there are harsh lights, noises, disturbing influences or hostility, the link may not be made. At best the clairvoyant may be extraordinarily accurate; at worst messages may be vague generalizations or meaningless rubbish; °extrasensory perception; °second sight; °telepathy.

Clark, Wilfred (1898–). Retired newspaper editor and founder of the *Wheel of British Yoga*, a movement which provides a link between °yoga groups in Great Britain and English-speaking countries overseas. He is the UK member on the All India Board of Yoga; °ill. 16.

16. Wilfred Clark

coincidence. Notable occurrence of events or circumstances without apparent causal connection. According to °astrology and the law of °karma all events are preordained and, when they occur simultaneously or if people meet as if by accident, these are part of the universal plan.

College of Psychic Studies, The. Founded by the Rev. W.S. °Moses, a Church of England vicar who was also its first president. The object of the College is to synthesize all branches of the °psychic, many of which seem incompatible with each other, and 'to investigate, study and classify psychic phenomena'. The membership is world wide, for it is neither a spiritualist centre nor a religious organization. Many eminent men and women have lectured and worked in study groups, among them °Lodge, Algernon Blackwood, °Cummins and Sir George Trevelyan, for it is a focal point for investigators, no matter what their beliefs. The library contains 11,000 volumes on all aspects of °extra-sensory perception and the College publishes *Light*, a quarterly journal containing articles, reviews and discussions on psychic matters. The President is Paul Beard and the Secretary is Barbara Somers.

colours. It used to be a °superstition that colours were merely lucky or unlucky, but it has now been proved that they are produced by °vibrations and, either directly or in combination with music, can be used to help with therapy in hospitals and mental asylums. Their significance in home and office decoration, and in clothing should always be borne in mind.

comet. A celestial body moving about the Sun in an elongated elliptical or parabolic orbit and consisting of a star-like nucleus surrounded with misty light and followed by a train of light or tail. Soothsayers usually make °prophecies when comets are due, but as they are not planets which make regular orbits they do not enter into astrological calculations.

conscious mind. The aware mind that takes note of processes and events in the living organism; a sense that develops to meet the needs of the external world. In °yoga it is also an assimilative process, sometimes acting as a sixth sense. It is not the whole mind but only a duality or property of the mind; °subconscious; °superconscious; °unconscious.

Coué, Emile (1857–1926). Psychotherapist, born in Troyes, France. Studied the use of °hypnotism and suggestion under H. Bernheim and A.A. Liébault, and established his own practice in 1910. Made his patients repeat daily the sentence: 'Every day and in every way I am becoming better and better.' His psychotherapeutic method, which was based on imagination, was highly successful. Repetition of the sentence sank into the °subconscious, eliminating ideas causing disease and distress. Coué stressed that he was not a healer but taught others to heal themselves. He claimed, however, to be able to effect organic changes by means of suggestion and had an enormous following mainly in France, the USA and Britain.

coven. A gathering, especially of °witches.

Crookes, Sir William (1832–1919). A pioneer physicist who specialized in radio and electrical problems and wrote books on a wide variety of subjects. He discovered thallium in 1861, invented the radiometer in 1875, discovered radiant matter in 1879, investigated the properties of radium and invented the spinthariscope. He was a founder member of the °Society for Psychical Research

17. Sir William Crookes

and was awarded the Order of Merit; °ill. 17.

Crowley, Edward Alexander (1875–1947). Known as Aleister Crowley, he was the son of wealthy Plymouth Brethren parents, educated at Malvern, Tonbridge and Trinity College, Cambridge. Travelled widely in Europe and Asia, was a mountaineer and dilettante who dabbled in °black °magic. He was versed in astrology and practised °Yi King and, as far as is known, never perverted anyone, though he called himself the Great Beast and was described by some as 'the wickedest man in the world'. Dedicated to the °occult, he produced such books as *Magick In Theory and Practice* and *Liber 777*; °ill. 18.

18. Aleister Crowley

Crumbine, Dr Samuel (1860–1959). An American physician who conducted scores of experiments in °hypnosis. He sent subjects into °trances during which they were able to see what some of his friends, 300 miles away, were doing. The movements of these people were constantly checked by telephone and were accurately described by the subject, proving that while under °hypnosis a person may be telepathic. Crumbine, who lived to nearly 100, was the first American physician to practise hypnosis effectively on his patients; °telepathy.

crystal gazing. The art of gazing into a crystal ball in order to see future events, a gift possessed only by sensitives. The idea that an actual picture appears in the ball like a colour film bears no relation to fact. The mind focuses on the crystal and images appear in the mind of the gazer, the crystal being merely a °medium on which to impinge thoughts. At first a milky mist appears, which bursts into a luminous, bluish field and on this background °visions appear. Faces and scenes develop, followed by movement, and the past or future unfolds. Though crystal gazing arouses much scepticism, reliable witnesses have testified to events seen in the crystal coming to pass.

Cummins, Geraldine (?–1969). Author of *The Scripts of Cleophas*, *They Survive* and *The Road To*

Immortality, which were the products of °influenced writing. She also wrote successful plays and was known as a °medium of integrity.

curse. The idea that words spoken in anger or in a spirit of revenge can harm seems so preposterous that many rational men reject the idea. Cursing is based on the theory that °vibrations emitted under certain conditions can harm or bring benefit. So many curses have proved effective in the past that, to the objective observer, their tragic results seem more than mere °coincidence. In Africa and India there have been numerous instances of curses taking effect, which baffle scientific investigation. In the past the Church cursed by bell, book and candle, and in September 1973 the Rev. Harold Cheales of St Laurence in Wyck, England, placed a curse on a man who stole church property, using a little-known service for the first day of Lent, called Commination, which contains 10 curses against wrongdoers and allows the priest to add a few of his own!

D

daemon. Evil spirit; demon; a being of a nature intermediate between that of God and Man; an inferior divinity or spirit; sometimes the soul of a person who has passed over, or an attendant spirit, or a malignant being of superhuman nature; a devil.

d'Arpentigny, Casimir Stanislaus (1798–?). He served under Napoleon at the siege of Danzig. He had such beautiful hands that he constantly compared them with those of the courtiers of Louis XVIII and originated the art of °chirognomy. He laid great emphasis on the thumb as being an index of talent and genius. He wrote *La Chirognomonie* and then *Le Science de la Main* which, after his death, °Desbarolles incorporated in his own *Almanac de la Main* and added it to his *Journal de Chiromancie*, finally publishing his great work *Révélations Complètes*. Between them, these two men almost transformed a discredited art into a science.

David-Neel, Alexandra (1869–1969). French author, traveller and authority on Tibet and Tibetan °yoga. Her books include *My Journey to Lhasa*, *Initiation and Initiates in Tibet*, *The Superman Life of Gesar Ling*, *Tibetan Journey* and *With Mystics and Magicians in Tibet*; °ill. 19.

Dee, Dr John (1527–1608). Born in Mortlake, England; graduate of Trinity College, Cambridge; an authority on Euclid; experimented

Delphic oracle

19. Alexandra David-Neel

with mirrors, prisms and lenses. Edward VI gave him a pension and a clerical living but Queen Mary persecuted him for practising the °occult. He drew up Elizabeth I's °horoscope and selected 14 January 1559 for her coronation; he became her intelligencer and she took no important step without consulting him. His great triumph was his °prediction of the approach of the Spanish Armada and the areas it was likely to attack. In his declining years Dee was made Warden of Christ's College, Manchester. James I, who did not believe in the °occult, however, feared Dee's powers and demanded that he be tried for °witchcraft, but nothing came of it. Predicted his own death at the age of 81 and just before his death the Angel Gabriel is said to have brought him a message of good cheer; °ill. 20.

20. Dr John Dee

Delphic oracle. Herodotus gives many examples of °oracles in Ancient Greece, the most famous being that at Delphi, where Pythia, the priestess, was thought to be the mouthpiece of Apollo. She was said to be possessed by the god, but there is little doubt that she was an unusually sensitive °medium. Plutarch said that the god merely put ideas or °visions into her mind and her own intelligence translated them into reality. In Greece no important affair of state was put into operation without first consulting the °oracle. Pythia chewed laurel leaves which induced a °trance, inhaled a hypnotic vapour which rose from a cleft in the temple floor, sank into a deep °trance and gave answers, usually in verse and often in the form of conundrums. Some maintain that the °trance was epileptiform, others that it was purely mediumistic. °Oracles were regarded as the voices of the highest wisdom in Greece, and Delphi became known as the 'navel of the world'.

demon. °Daemon; °dervish.

demonic possession. Possession of person or animal by °daemon; °obsession.

dense body. The physical body; °etheric body; °linga sharira.

dervish. A Muslim °fakir or °yogi who has taken a vow of poverty and adopted an ascetic life. At times dervishes are overcome by frenzied °ecstasy, induced by whirling round repeatedly; when their bodies are supposed to be possessed by °daemons, and they sometimes stab themselves or even kill others.

Desbarolles, Adrian Adolf (1801–1886). A Parisian painter who, when jilted at the age of 35, gave up painting, turned to °palmistry and travelled in Spain, where he met a gipsy who so astounded him with her °predictions that he devoted the remainder of his life to the study of the hand. In 1859 he wrote *Les Mystères de la Main*, which sold 22 editions and brought him wealth and fame.

Devil, the. In Jewish and Christian theology the supreme spirit of evil; the tempter and spiritual enemy of mankind; the foe of God and holiness; Satan. The Devil is an integral part of most orthodox religions. Without the evil generated by him there could be no contrasting good, or salvation. Generally he is depicted with horns, cleft hooves and a forked tail. At a general audience at the Vatican recently, Pope Paul VI referred to him as 'an invisible presence, an obscure agent and enemy, and evil is not merely a spiritual deficiency but an efficiency; a living being, spiritual, perverted and a perverter; a terrible reality, mysterious and fearful'. Under the name Lucifer he tried to dethrone God but was banished to Hell by Michael and his angels; °daemon; °devil dancers; °devil worship.

devil dancers. Sects in Africa, China, S. America and the East. The dancer's body becomes possessed by the °Devil and he goes into a cataleptic °trance, leaps and whirls, passes skewers through his cheeks

21. The devil dancers of Yare, Venezuela, caper through the streets of the small town at the feast of Corpus Christi

and performs feats needing superhuman strength. Possession is self-induced and, when the evil °spirit leaves the body, the dancer collapses and lies exhausted, often for hours; °sungma; °ill. 21.

Devil worshippers. Sects which for quite logical reasons pay homage to the °Devil. They maintain that, as he has immense power to harm, it is politic to mollify him in this life. God, they argue, is merciful and will forgive transgressors after death, thus enabling sinners to enter heaven if they exhibit remorse. The °Devil, however, will avenge himself on those who have spurned him while on earth, so it is as well to seek his favour. The best-known sect is the Yezidis, who are a mixture of Arab and Kurd, and live in the Sinjar hills of Northern Iraq. They believe that God is only interested in heavenly affairs and has appointed the °Devil to rule over the earth for 10,000 years. They refer to him as Melek Taus, the Peacock King. Their creed is an admixture of tenets from the Talmud, the Bible and the Koran and their holy books are Kitab el Eswed (the Black Book), Kitab el Jalwek (a proclamation of allegiance to Satan) and the Book of Revelation. The founder of the religion of this gentle, hospitable people was Sheikh Adi Ben Mousafer, who was born in Baalbek, Lebanon in AD 585.

de Wohl, Louis (1902–1961). Famous Austrian astrologer who at one time advised Hitler but, seeing events in the dictator's chart and disagreeing with his tyranny, he escaped to Britain, where Lord Halifax introduced him into the War Office. He was given the rank of captain in the army and was unofficial astrologer to the Cabinet. He foretold Wavell's success in North Africa, the victory of Matapan and, after comparing the charts of Rommel and Montgomery, he predicted that Montgomery would triumph. He also said that Hitler would not invade Britain. His novels include *Secret Service of The Sky*, *I Follow My Stars*, *Commonsense Astrology* and a number of novels; °astrology.

divination. Insight into or discovery of the unknown or future by supernatural means; °Book of Fate.

divining. °Dowsing.

Dixon, Jeane. Currently one of the best-known female seers in the USA; she does not go into a °trance but is a true °psychic. Has dictated books about herself and her °prophecies, e.g. *My Life and Prophecies*, though some of the most recent writing seems tinged with wishful thinking.

Dowden, Hester. According to °Cummins, Dowden, the daughter of Prof. Edward Dowden of Trinity College, Dublin, was the finest °automatist since °Piper, a medium of the front rank. She wrote literary articles for the *Athenaeum* and two books, *Psychic Messages From Oscar Wilde* and *Voices From The Void*. She could have earned her living as a concert pianist but, encouraged by °Barrett, she subjected herself to exacting tests, came through successfully and devoted her life to psychical research. On the evening of the sinking of the 'Lusitania' she was operating a °ouija board which spelt out a message, relayed to those present by the Rev. Savill Hicks, that Sir Hugh Lane (the great authority on pictures, who was a passenger) had been drowned. This was only one of scores of accurate messages; °psychic.

Dowding, H. T. C. Lord (1882–1970). On retiring from the service, Air Chief Marshal Lord Dowding investigated °psychic phenomena, collaborated with °mediums and supervised tests under stringent conditions. He became convinced that some form of life existed after death. Wrote *Many Mansions*, *Lychgate* and *Dark Star*.

dowsing. The art of finding (divining) water, oil, metals or minerals by means of a hazel twig, metal rod or °radionics machine. The diviner holds the two arms of a Y-shaped hazel twig with the third end pointing down and forwards. When passing over an area where the substance sought lies, the free end of the twig or rod jerks upwards, indicating its presence. Dowsers can also operate successfully on maps thousands of miles from the substances they seek and George de la Warr, at the request of the Indian Government, discovered a vast pocket of methane gas in the Himalayas by divining on a map in Oxford.

Doyle, Sir Arthur Conan (1859–1930). An Irish doctor of medicine and creator of the famous character Sherlock Holmes, who gave up medicine to become one of the most successful authors of his day. He was the first to write detective fiction in which crimes were solved entirely from clues by a process of deduction. He became absorbed in °spiritualism and the °psychic generally. His photographs of fairies for instance were greeted with scepticism. He and °Lodge were associated in many investigations into the °occult; °thought photography.

dreams, prophetic. From the earliest times it has been recognized that dreams have meanings, and some are prophetic though there is no scientific method of interpreting them. Some dreams have shown that the future is already laid out and the conventional limits we place on time do not exist. The Bible gives many instances of prophetic dreams and innumerable dreams have been recorded in our time that have accurately foretold future events; °prophecy.

Drown, Dr Ruth. A chiropractor in Los Angeles who improved and refined the °Abrams Box and developed a camera to photograph organs and tissues of patients, using nothing but a drop of blood, even though the subjects were many miles distant. It also took pictures in cross-section, which cannot be done by X-rays. Though this pioneer of °radionics was granted a British patent for her apparatus, her claim was denounced by the FDA as originating in the realms of science fiction and her equipment was confiscated in the 1940s. She was stigmatized in *Life* magazine as a charlatan and died of grief, but left behind *Theory and Techniques of Radio Therapy*, probably the first book in the English language on the subject. Her work was carried on, however, by G. W. Wigglesworth of Chicago and his brother, an electronics engineer, who developed an improved device known as a 'pathoclast' or disease-breaker, and then

Druids

22. The Druid stones of Stenness, Orkney

founded the Pathometric Association.

Druids. No one knows exactly when the cult of the Druids and °sun worship began, but Dr Churchward, the anthropologist, believes that the Druids were taught by Egyptian priests who landed in Ireland and the West of England. Others maintain that their teachings sprang from Pythagoras, who was taught the mysteries by the Brahmins, and he in turn taught the °kelts. Druids believe in the evolution of the °soul from the lowest animal forms to humanity and beyond, and in °karma, death being just a passage to another life. It is thought that the Druids of Ancient Gaul and Britain date back to about 200 BC, 1,000 years after the greater part of Stonehenge was erected, and they probably had a hand in its completion. In order to establish an almanac, they raised monoliths such as those at Aldborough near York, the circles of stones near Keswick, and used Stonehenge as an observatory-temple. According to Moses Cotsworth their observatories usually consisted of circles of 30 stones to equal the 30-day monthly gauges of the solar year. They did not indulge in blood 'sacrifices; °ill. 22.

dryad. Nymph thought to inhabit trees; wood nymph; the term includes the dryads and hamadryads of classical times. Mythology says

39

that when a tree dies the spirit that inhabits it dies too.

Dryden, John (1631–1700). Poet Laureate. He believed in the °occult and practised °astrology. When his wife was about to have her first child, he laid his watch on the table beside her and asked the midwife to make a note of the exact time of the birth. After calculating the °horoscope, he said, 'And in grief I speak, he was born in an evil hour; Jupiter, Venus and Sun were all under the earth, and the lord of his ascendant afflicted by a hateful square of Mars and Saturn. If he lives to arrive at his 8th year he will go near to a violent death, but if he should escape, as I see but small hope, he will in his 23rd year be under the same evil direction; and if he should, which seems impossible, escape also that, the 33rd or 34th year is, I fear . . .' The boy was terribly injured by a stag on his 8th birthday but recovered. In Cambridge, when he was 23, he had a severe fall and suffered badly as a result; he was 34 years old when he was drowned while swimming in the Thames at Datchet.

Dukes, Sir Paul (1889–1967). One of the best-known British exponents and interpreters of °yoga. Was employed in secret service work for Britain, for which he was knighted. His interest in °yoga was aroused in Russia and fostered in America. His feet had been badly frostbitten in Russia and °yoga improved his health and changed his entire outlook. He taught, demonstrated and wrote books on °yoga, first at the Legat School with Nadine Nicolaeva-Legat and later with Diana Fitzgerald, whom he married and who now runs a °yoga school in South Africa. He retained his physical vigour and mental alertness well into his eighties, when he died in a car crash.

Dunne, John William (1875–1949). Mathematician and aeronautical engineer. At the age of 6 he was bedridden by an accident and spent 3 years on his back, during which time he spent hours indulging in metaphysical speculation. When he was 19 he started to investigate °spiritualism and on 3 occasions received significant messages from a being he called 'the angel'. He frequently dreamed of events thousands of miles away, as they were taking place. His best-known °dream, that of the volcanic disaster in Martinique, was accurate except for one detail: 40,000 inhabitants were engulfed in lava, but he saw only 4,000. Details of his °dreams are given in *An Experiment With Time* and his theory that time is a regressive concept is explained in *The Serial Universe*, *The New Immortality* and *Nothing Dies*. He was probably the first distinguished man who tried scientifically to prove the survival of consciousness after death.

E

ecstasy. Rapture; extreme concentration of attention amounting to semi-trance, as a phenomenon or phase of prolonged contemplation of a limited field, particularly of religious °mysticism; a state of self-hypnosis achieved by drugs, violent dancing or other movements producing cataleptic conditions; °hypnosis; °trance.

ectoplasm. From the Greek *ecto* (outer) and *plasm* (mould or matrix). Firm outer layer of an amoeba or the like; in °spiritualism, a form of plasma. Till recently science recognized only 3 states of matter: solids, liquids and gases. Now a fourth state has been added called plasmas, which are streams of masses of ionized molecules which in many respects resemble gases, though they do not expand indefinitely. They form the white hot glow round arc-lights, the glow round the sun, and the earth's ionosphere. Man-made plasmas are temporary and return to the gaseous state when electric current is switched off, whereas space plasmas are permanent and in thermodynamic equilibrium, and they are better conductors of electricity than solids, liquids and gases. The matter produced when a spiritual body is materialized consists of a form known as ectoplasm. It is a part of the °etheric body and is drawn upon to furnish a temporary vehicle for some entity in the astral world wishing to make contact with the physical world, as explained in *Reality of Physical Phenomena* by W. J. Crawford; °astral body; °astral projection.

Eddy family, the. Their mother, Julia Macomb, was a °medium descended from a long line of °mediums, one of whom had been burnt as a °witch. Neighbours consulted her when they lost articles and she found them. She married Zephanniah Eddy and all their children were °mediums. When Zephanniah discovered this, he whipped them so brutally that the blood ran down their bodies. He allowed a friend, Anson Ladd, to pour scalding water over the back of his son William and burn coals on his head to exorcise the °Devil. Eventually the °spirits materialized and forced Zephanniah to leave the house. In 1874 °Olcott decided to investigate the Eddys' ability to materialize °spirits, which they did in full view of 10 observers. Under strict conditions they: 1. materialized human forms; 2. materialized hands of men, women and children, some mutilated and showing evidence of amputation; 3. the detached hands wrote the names of deceased persons; 4. one of the Eddys played music on instruments requiring at least 4 musicians whereas he was the only one in the cabinet; 5. caused the appearance of several hundreds of °spirits during the 3 weeks °Olcott was at their farm, many of whom were recognized by those present; 6. the °spirits spoke Chinese, German, Finnish, Scandinavian, Georgian, Arabic, Red Indian dialects and other languages, though the Eddy boys had only primary education. °Olcott weighed one °spirit four times within several minutes and found the weight varied from 65–88lbs. The weight of another °spirit varied from 52–77lbs within minutes. The °medium through which these °spirits were produced weighed 175lbs but no explanation could be given at the time for these divergencies in weight. Towards the end of extended tests °Blavatsky arrived and one of her dead uncles materialized, dressed in tails with a black ribbon round his neck from which hung the Cross of St Anne. The °spirit guide then approached her and said, 'I am about to give you a test of the genuineness of these manifestations. It should satisfy you and a sceptical world. I hand you the medal of honour worn by your late father, which was buried with his body in Russia.' With which a medal awarded to officers in the Turkish campaign of 1828 was produced.

Eddy, Mary Baker (1821–1910). Born in Bow, Concord, USA, she was the sixth child of Congregationalist parents. Though illness limited her early education, she read widely and wrote poetry. She suffered from a spinal disease, became preoccupied with questions of health and experimented with osteopathy. She then heard of Phineas Quimby, who wrought remarkable cures without medicine or surgery, and was cured by him. She thought he had rediscovered the healing methods of Jesus, so she studied his notes and lectured on his theories. After Quimby's death she had a bad fall and was medically judged incurable, but she turned to the New Testament, studied it and was restored to health. That was the start of °Christian Science. She took students and her fortunes improved. She published *Science and Health*, which was enlarged to *Science and Health With a Key To the Scriptures*, and in 1877 married (for the third time) Asa G. Eddy, one of her disciples. She founded the *Christian Science Journal*, *Christian Science Sentinel* and the daily paper the *Christian*

Science Monitor.

Edwards, Harry (1893–). From Burrows Lea, Surrey, England, he is probably the most widely publicized °psychic healer in Britain. Cures by laying on of hands and by °absent healing. Has restored to health incurables for whom the medical profession could do nothing. Though hymns are sung at his meetings, it is claimed that his cures are not brought about by faith – many sceptics have been cured – but by a power that flows from his hands into their bodies.

egrigor. A thought form. Occultists believe that as we think we create in the world of the mind an intangible and invisible pattern or formation which persists, and if concentration is intense enough this thought form can be photographed and, in rare instances, even materialized; °Serios; °thought photography; °tulpa.

ekisha. Name given to any Japanese pavement fortune-teller who combines °astrology with °palmistry. Cleft sticks are also studied to evaluate chances of °predictions being fulfilled.

elemental. In ancient philosophy there are 4 elements: earth, water, air and fire, and an elemental is a body composed or produced by one or more of these elements. Elementalism is a worship of one of these elements, e.g. fire worship. In the °occult, elementals are °spirits that are neither men nor °angels, neither good nor bad; they live long but are not immortal.

elf. °Spirit in dwarf form supposed to possess supernatural powers; °nature spirit. A belief in elves persists in Iceland, where records have been preserved of their nature and habits. Though their bodies are composed of tenuous matter they are invisible, except to sensitives. Many Icelanders believe that they can communicate with elves during sleep, and that these little people are the unwashed children of Eve who, when visited by Jehovah, showed Him only her washed children and hid the others. Elves enjoy food, make their own wine and a few Icelanders claim to have witnessed their religious worship. They should not be confused with trolls who are dull and even stupid.

Enochian system. A rich repository of eschatological lore and teaching. Jewish legend attributed the invention of writing, arithmetic, astronomy and °astrology to the prophet Enoch; °eschatology; °tablets of I'sid'i.

eschatology. The doctrine of death, judgement, heaven and hell. To a materialist it is a science without foundation; °Enochian system; °tablets of I'sid'i.

Esdaille, James (1805–1859). Scots surgeon who, while in charge of a special hospital near Calcutta in 1845, performed his first operation by hypnotizing a patient. He then amputated the arm of a Brahmin without him feeling the slightest pain, removed a mass weighing 80lbs from another patient and a tumour weighing 8 stone from a third one. In 8 months he performed 261 major, and hundreds of minor, operations, using only °hypnotism as an anaesthetic, and reduced the death rate of patients from 50 to 5 per cent. The medical profession tried to discredit him and the Medical College in Calcutta tried to suppress his methods. Only when the press came to his rescue and the Viceroy, Lord Dalhousie, promoted him did he gain any recognition; °hypnosis; °hypnotism.

esoteric. Designed for, or appropriate to, an inner circle of disciples; communicated to or intelligible by the initiated only; °Rosicrucians; °yoga.

ESP. °Extra-sensory perception; °psi.

ether. That substance which forms the 4 higher or finer sub-planes of the physical world: 1. first etheric or atomic; 2. second etheric or subatomic; 3. third etheric or superetheric; 4. fourth etheric.

etheric body. Built of finer physical matter than the °dense body, invisible and intangible, but upon which the physical body depends for its flow of vitality and its sense-consciousness; °ether.

etheric double. The counterpart of the °dense body, pervading and sustaining it, formed in the matter of the 4 etheric sub-planes; °ether; °linga-sharira.

etheric plane. Comprised of the 4 etheric sub-planes of the physical world; °ether.

exorcism. The action of expelling an evil °spirit by adjuration, as opposed to conjuration or the ceremony observed in calling up °spirits. Dr A.T. Schofield, the eminent psychiatrist, said, 'Possession by an evil spirit is tacitly recognized by most of our alienists.' The affected person goes into a rigid cataleptic state and utters the most fearsome blasphemies or may even commit a heinous crime, such as murder, without being aware of it. Priests overcome °demonic possession by prayer, worship and sacrament, by sprinkling holy water and anointing with oil.

extra-sensory perception. Usually abbreviated to ESP or °psi, the twenty-third letter of the Greek alphabet, and now used to describe the psychic in general, i.e. phenomena and experiences for which there are no rational explanations.

eye, third. Known to the Ancient Egyptians and the °yogis. According to some authorities it is sited between and slightly above the normal two, is the seat of all thought and marvellous powers are attributed to it. Generally associated with the pineal gland. Sometimes known as the middle eye. In Greek mythology Cyclops had a single middle eye.

face reading

When the third eye is enlarged and unusually powerful, the owner is always °psychic, clairvoyant and extremely intuitive; °clairvoyance.

F

face reading. °Physiognomy.
fadic number. Magic number of destiny; °numerology.
fairy. A belief in some form of diminutive and graceful humanoid creature has existed for centuries. When Mrs Kim Mzyk of Meir, England, said she saw a fairy at the bottom of her garden, 300 people wrote to a newspaper to say that they too had seen fairies. There used to be a British Fairy Society in Lydd, Kent. E.L. Gardner and °Doyle investigated fairies seen by two children in a glen in Cottingley in the Scottish Highlands and took photographs of them, which were published in *Strand* magazine of December 1920. The children, both clairvoyant, played with the fairies and densified their subtle, cloudlike bodies, enabling them to be photographed. Stringent checks were made on the photographic plates to detect fraud, and later Gardner wrote a book called *Fairies*. So many people claim to have seen them that their existence should be seriously considered; °leprechaun.

faith healing. Cures wrought through prayer and faith. Lourdes is the European centre of faith healing. Each year thousands of sick, maimed and crippled people flock to the town where they pray, sing hymns, are blessed and dipped in holy water. Scores return cured and the discarded crutches are piled high for all to see. Whether prayer, holy water and the °vibrations of the crowds accomplish the cures, or whether they are caused by self-hypnosis, none can say. The medical profession is unwilling to commit itself, though individuals such as Dr Alexis °Carrel and Dr Christopher Woodard are convinced that prayer and faith are the healing instruments; °hypnosis.

fakir (faquir). A Muslim religious

fatalism

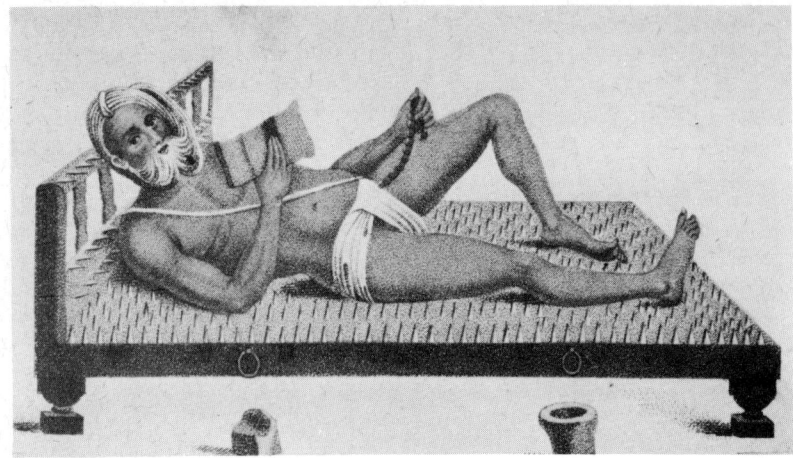

23. A Hindu fakir on his bed of nails

mendicant, though the term is now applied to all naked ascetics, °mystics and °yogis who sit for a lifetime on beds of nails, run skewers through their cheeks or indulge in other forms of self-immolation in the belief that by so doing they will gain merit and achieve °nirvana; °ill. 23.

fatalism. The belief that every action and event is predetermined by arbitrary decree; submission to all that happens as inevitable. It is common to confuse fatalism with °karma.

faun. °Spirit of animal life; the *fauni*, *panes* and *sylvani* of the Romans; the *satyri* of the Greeks; usually represented by men with horns and the tail and legs of a goat; once worshipped by shepherds and farmers.

fetish. An object having magical properties or animated by a °spirit. Fetishes are used all over Africa, in New Guinea and the West Indies by °witch-doctors and °voodoo men to gain power over those they wish to control. There are good fetishes and bad; the good fetish is given to one whom the °ju-ju man wishes to protect, but it will work only if it is stronger than an evil fetish that has already been laid on him. Much depends on the powers of the respective witch doctors. Though there is no scientific explanation for the way in which fetishes work, that they are effective is based on the evidence of innumerable reliable witnesses

fire-walking. Walking barefoot

fire walking

through a trench paved with burning charcoal and logs. The art is practised in India, Africa, South America, the West Indies and Malaysia. In Malaysia fire walkers demonstrate their immunity by playing soccer barefoot, with red-hot hollow iron balls! Under the tutelage of experts, many Europeans claim to have walked through fire

24. Fire-walking at the festival of Kali Mai Puja, Guyana

successfully. Dr John Hill, Professor of Biblical History at the University of California, was invited by a chief in Tahiti to traverse a 100-foot trench lined with red-hot stones. He was assured that he would not be burned and, though he emerged unscathed, the heat was so intense that several days later the skin on his face peeled off. Dr Brigham, an American scientist, stated that when a volcano erupted in Napoopoo, Hawaii, 3 Polynesians invited him to walk over a 150-yard stretch of lava. On their assurance that he would not be harmed, he did so wearing boots. Halfway across his boots were burnt away but he continued unharmed, in bare feet. Sir James Frazer and other anthropologists regard this as a form of sympathetic °magic, but belief in immunity seems to be the essential ingredient; °ill. 24.

Flamel, Nicholas (1330–1418). British alchemist; °alchemy.

Flamsteed, John (1646–1719). First Astronomer Royal, whose chief work was a catalogue of the fixed stars. Like most scientists of his day, he was a competent astrologer. On one occasion an ignorant woman, confusing astronomy with °astrology, told him she had mislaid a bundle of linen and asked him where it was. Instead of scorning her, he drew up an horary chart and told her exactly where to find it.

Flint, Leslie. Currently one of the most successful British °mediums with the rare gift of independent direct voice. He has recorded hundreds of voices of the famous on tape: Oscar Wilde, Ellen Terry, Stephen Ward, Archbishop Cosmo Lang, Rudolf Valentino, George V, etc. He collaborated with °Dowding under strict test conditions.

floromancy. The belief that flowers possess feeling and will respond to sympathetic or brutal treatment like humans. Nearly a century ago Sir Jagdis Bose, the Indian scientist, proved that plants and flowers are affected by electric shocks, surgery and poisons, and Luther Burbank proved that plants have a sensitive nervous system and by talking to them one can create °vibrations of love. This, he claims, is why one person has green fingers whereas another cannot make anything grow. In 1972 Dr V. Pushkin, the Russian scientist, proved that plants have emotions by attaching an encephalograph to a geranium leaf and getting a hypnotized man to address pleasant and unpleasant words to it. The plant reacted exactly as a human being would. Plants should be grown and studied in relation to the planets, for each day has a different planetary association. The art of floromancy is the study of plants in relation to the planets, their environment, their reaction to music, and events likely to affect them. Flowers also radiate °vibra-

foot reading

tions and have the power to cure disease; °Bach.

foot reading. °Cartopedy; °solistry.

Forcas. Being who is credited in °black °magic with having power; °Beelzebub.

fortune-telling. Any means of seeing into the future and describing events: °astrology, °palmistry, °clairvoyance, etc.

Fox, George (1624–1691). Founder of the Society of Friends (Quakers); he was °psychic and had numerous clairvoyant experiences. In 1665, when he was in Lancaster Jail, he 'saw' the Lord's power turn against the Turks who threatened to overrun Christendom and a month later news arrived of their defeat. In 1666 he saw in a °vision the 'angel of the Lord with glittering sword' stretched southward and almost at once came the Black Death, followed by the Great Fire of London. He was persecuted by Cromwell but 'saw' the restoration of the monarchy 3 years before it happened. Fox cured scores of people by the laying-on of hands and, when a mad woman was brought to him, he said he made the Lord's power settle on her 'and she was mended'. He also cured one John Jay who was brought to him 'dead and with a broken neck'. In his journal are recorded many apparent miracles of healing brought about by him. Nor could enemies harm him. When someone armed a lunatic with birches and urged him to thrash Fox, Fox bade the man throw his rods into the fire, which he did. At Ulverston a mob set on him, broke an arm and knocked him unconscious, but it is recorded that on regaining consciousness he looked at his arm with the love he bore his persecutors, a power flowed through it and it was restored.

Fox, Margaret and Kate. The house in which they lived with their parents in Hydesville, New York State, USA, in 1847 was subject to bangings and knockings on the walls and doors for which there was no explanation. Eventually the noises were interpreted to mean numbers and letters which were translated into messages. Some force also moved heavy furniture. The sisters gave public demonstrations to prove they were °mediums and were championed by Horace Greely, the famous editor of the *New York Times*. In 1861 Kate Fox was brought to London by Charles Livermore, where °Crookes wrote after testing her: 'For power and certainty I have met no one at all approached by Miss Kate Fox. For months I enjoyed almost limitless opportunities of testing the various phenomena occurring in the presence of this lady. With full knowledge of the various theories which have been started off, chiefly in America, to explain the sounds, I have tested them in every way until there has been no escape from the conviction that they were true objective occurrences not produced by trickery or mechanical means.' They were the pioneers of modern °spiritualism and an account of their work is given in *The Unwilling Martyrs* by Mrs Pond.

Franklin, Benjamin (1706–1790). Printer, postmaster, politician, scientist, philosopher and diplomat, was one of the greatest Americans of his time. He was well versed in °astrology and while at college he drew up the °horoscope of a fellow student named Titus Leeds, whom he calculated would die at 3.20 pm on 7 October 1753 at the conjunction of Sun and Mercury. Leeds died at the exact time predicted, but this was put down to °coincidence. Franklin was also a prominent °Rosicrucian.

freak. A monstrosity of any species; denoting something abnormal or capriciously irregular. It has been found that 1 person in 10 has freakish tendencies, that is, he/she departs in some way from the normal even as little as being left-handed or wearing glasses. Sensitives and °mediums come into this category. Many phenomena that cannot be explained are termed freakish: Brian Williams had merely to hold an electric light bulb in his hands for it to light up; Kuda Bux could ride a bicycle through thick traffic though his eyes were covered by clay and bound; Frank Kittler and Jan Zysak had merely to hold hands to turn themselves into a radio receiver; Jack Ducamp of Dalhart, Texas, turned himself into a short-wave radio station at Monterey each evening, whether he wished to or not. After death a medical examination revealed that Ducamp's skull contained a number of fine membranes which responded to electrical disturbances at a wavelength of about 30 metres.

Freud, Sigmund (1856–1939). Originator of the therapeutics of neurotic diseases. He suggested that most neurotic diseases are due to a conflict between the °unconscious and conscious parts of the mind: the conscious endeavouring to act in conformity with social training, while the °unconscious tries to find an outlet for primitive tendencies suppressed by the patient. By gradually bringing the suppressed material into consciousness, so that the patient understands his mental conflict, the symptoms should disappear. Freud founded the system of treatment known as psychoanalysis, which he applied more often than not to the investigation of °dreams, as he considered these to represent in a symbolic manner the gratification of suppressed wishes. He wrote innumerable books and papers on the subject and is now known as the father of psychoanalysis.

Fuller, Curtis (1912–   ). Born in

the USA. In 1948 he and an associate started *Fate* magazine which now has the largest circulation of any °occult periodical in the world.

G

Gall, Franz Joseph (1758–1828). He became interested in faces at the age of 9, when he found that boys with prominent eyes could learn their lessons by heart much more easily than others. He also found that certain features corresponded to certain talents and that the shape of the skull seemed to determine character and ability. After graduating, he worked in schools, prisons and lunatic asylums. When a doctor at the prison in Graetz sent him a box of skulls, he picked up one and said: 'This is the head of a thief!' He was right. He believed that the shape of the skull determined the man. Later he collaborated with °Spurzheim to give the new learning a scientific basis; °phrenology.

Gandhi, Sir Motilal K. (1929–). A Jain born in Bombay who practises °astrology in London, specializing in the horary side. He has publicly made a number of political and economic °predictions that have come true. He uses the Jain system, which differs in some respects from the Hindu, used widely in India, and even more from the traditional European system; °ill. 25.

Garland, Hamblin. Author and member of the American Academy of Arts and Letters; disciple of Herbert Spencer; an agnostic and evolutionist, who started an investigation into °spiritualism in 1891 after reading Alfred Russel Wallace, who believed in the °psychic. He also investigated °psychometry, impersonation without °trance, °spirit writing and other aspects of

25. Sir Motilal K. Gandhi

°psi. His integrity and position made him one of the foremost investigators of his day and his *Forty Years of Psychical Research* is one of the first authentic works on the subject.

Garrett, Eileen (1893–1968). Born in Eire of Irish and Polish parents. One of the great °mediums. Her gift was apparent at a very early age when she 'saw' a cousin who had died and subsequently had conversations with 2 girls and a boy who were her constant companions. She travelled widely and edited a magazine devoted to °spiritualism. She worked in New York under the auspices of the Society for Psychical Research and then at Duke University, under Professor Hyslop, Dr Franklin Prince, Prof. Gardner Murphy and William McDougal, where she demonstrated °telepathy, °clairvoyance and °astral projection under test conditions arranged by a psychoanalyst in New York and a physician in Newfoundland. In 1951 she founded the Parapsychology Foundation and was the first editor of the *Parapsychology Review*. *Adventures in The Supernormal* and *My Life As a Search For The Meaning of Mediumship* by her, give details of her remarkable career; °parapsychology; °ill. 26.

26. Eileen Garrett

Geller, Uri. An Israeli who is best known for his TV exhibitions of spoon-bending and for his powers, under test conditions, of seeing objects even though they are covered, placed in boxes or in adjacent rooms. Some power – probably electric – emanates from his body, which can stop watches or bend their hands, though they may be miles away. Prof. Hasted of Birkbeck College, London, said: 'If you take a battery and short-circuit it across a geiger counter, it has the same effect as Geller. He seems to be electric. He is like an electric eel.' Dr A. Puharich, a member of the New York Academy of Science and the American Association for the Advancement of Science, who has carried out a series of controlled tests with Geller, says that Geller claims to get his powers from an extra-terrestrial intelligence, which has programmed him for an import-

Geller

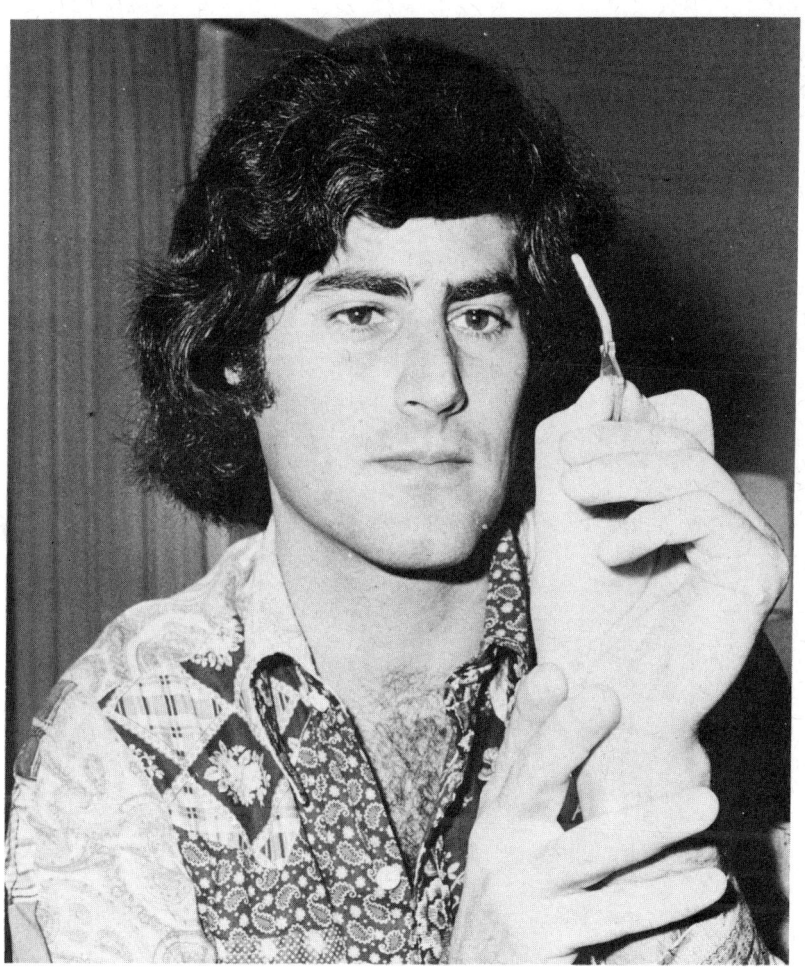

27. Uri Geller bending a key

ant task on earth for years to come. Prof. Taylor of King's College, London, says that, when Geller was placed in front of a geiger counter, 'it showed 500 times above background', which means he is so full of radioactivity that the building should be evacuated on grounds of

gem

safety! Further tests are being carried out in England and in America to find out exactly what this power is; °ill. 27.

gem. Precious or semi-precious stone. Every object, living or inanimate, radiates °vibrations which affect those who come into contact with them. The °vibrations from some gems are lucky to their wearers and the rays from others are supposed to harm; for instance, the opal is supposed to bring bad luck to all except those born under the planet Libra; °birth stone; °charms.

Geoff, the talking mongoose. In the 1930s R.S. Lambert, editor of the *Listener*, and °Price investigated the case of a talking mongoose in Ireland called Geoff. Lambert wrote an account corroborating the fact that the mongoose spoke and as a result his sanity was questioned. He sued and was awarded £7,500 in damages.

ghost. The °soul or °spirit; an incorporeal body or being; the soul of a deceased person spoken of as inhabiting the unseen world.

Ghost Society. Founded in Cambridge, England, in 1851 to conduct scientific inquiry into the supernatural by E.W. Benson (later Archbishop of Canterbury), °Sidgwick and others.

ghoul. Derived from the Arabic *ghul* (to seize). An evil °spirit, originally in Arab countries, which robbed graves and preyed on corpses. The cult spread to West Africa where Muslim influence is strong, and with the slave trade to the West Indies, where it has been incorporated in °voodoo.

ginseng. Plant of the species Aralia or Panax found in Korea, Manchuria, North China and the USA. Ginseng means 'man root' because the root resembles a human torso with arms. The Chinese variety is known as an *elixir vitae*, supposed to prolong life indefinitely and to have °occult properties. It is said that when uprooted it screams, sending men mad. It is a tranquillizer and soporific, and produces sweet dreams. The Russians give it to their cosmonauts to enable them to combat infectious diseases and General Westmoreland used to take ginseng tea for breakfast to enable him to deal with his daily problems in Vietnam. The Chinese say that ginseng, lying in the earth for countless ages, absorbs the vital substance of life and it was in the past reserved exclusively for their emperors.

gipsies. The exact origin of the gipsies is not known; some say it is India, other authorities say Egypt. India however, seems the most probable and, if so, they may have left the country in the 14th century, migrated to Egypt, scattered to the Balkans, Spain and France, and then to England. Scores of their words are Hindi, e.g. *bal* (hair), *bee bee* (aunt or woman), *burra-paanee* (ocean), *chhurree* (knife), *muchhee* (fish), *rawnee* or *ranee* (lady or queen). The true gipsy is usually °psychic and has the ability to see into the future, though not by reading the palm. The gipsy looks at a person and reads him while the gipsy's palm is crossed with silver to ward off evil, both for him and his client. True Romanies tell the time by the position of the sun and forecast the weather by the flight of birds. The best-known gipsy families in Britain are the Lees, Boswells and Petulengros.

glossolalia. A pseudo-type of language, elaborated in the recesses of the subconscious but generally supported by grammatical rules, making little sense and amounting to no more than a jumble of sounds.

glyph. The °magic glyph, evolved from a person's name and birth date, is supposed to be the most powerful of °occult devices, corresponding to the °talismans and °amulets of the Ancients. Each person can design his own glyph, the shape of which is the only real bringer of luck for him. If made correctly and used as a book-plate, °amulet, dress ornament, ring, seal, or other personal ornament, it should, according to ancient lore, protect the wearer from misfortune and ill-health. If it is set with the correct °birth stone and inscribed with his lucky number and zodiacal sign, its potency is vastly increased; °ill. 28.

Sun	☉
Moon	☽
Mercury	☿
Venus	♀
Mars	♂
Jupiter	♃
Saturn	♄
Uranus	♅
Neptune	♆
Pluto	♇ or ⯓

Aries	♈
Taurus	♉
Gemini	♊
Cancer	♋
Leo	♌
Virgo	♍
Libra	♎
Scorpio	♏
Sagittarius	♐
Capricorn	♑
Aquarius	♒
Pisces	♓

28. Glyphs for the signs of the zodiac, the sun, the moon and the planets

gnome, gnomide (female). Diminutive spirit of subterranean race guarding treasures of earth. Supposed to be similar to a °goblin in size, though not a °daemon.

gnostic. Member of a sect of Early Christians who claimed special °occult powers and said that Jesus was not a man, but of divine origin. They were influenced by Eastern °mysticism and their powers developed by °meditation and invocation of their former leader.

goblin. A mischievous and ugly °daemon of short stature.

Granth Sahib. '*Honourable Book*', the bible of the Sikhs, inspired by Baba °Nanak, their first °guru. Ten successive gurus or guides are the authors, each writing in the name °Nanak, for the °spirit of each Nanak gave his successor the wisdom contained in the book. The last of the earth °mediums, Gobind Singh, proved the power of predictive °clairvoyance by prophesying, 500 years ago, that there would be both Hindu and Muslim rulers in India, and the British would rule for a long time.

graphology. The study of handwriting; the art and science of inferring character, disposition and aptitudes from handwriting. Not an exact science, but one in which certain laws and rules are followed as in medicine, °palmistry and °astrology. Much is left to the skill and experience of the practitioners, but the readings of great exponents such as Dr Robert Saudek, a Czech who collaborated with the police and psychiatrists to determine criminal and other tendencies, and assisted employers to engage suitable staff, can be uncannily accurate. Graphologists do not predict future events.

Greatrakes, Valentine. From Waterford, Ireland, he discovered in 1662 that he had the power to cure the °king's evil (scrofula) by touching people. His fame spread so rapidly that the Earl of Orrery invited him to England to cure Lady Conway of a persistent headache, but he failed to give her relief. While at Ragley, Lord Conway's seat in Warwickshire, however, he cured a multitude. From there he moved to Worcester and then to Lincoln's Inn Fields, London, where he had enormous success, treating not only scrofula but also ague and other diseases.

Great Seal of the USA, the. The reverse of the Great Seal depicts a Masonic emblem because more than 50 of the signatories of the Declaration of Independence were either Masons or °Rosicrucians and were much concerned with the esoteric sciences such as °astrology, °numerology, °tarot, °Kabalah, etc. Benjamin °Franklin and Thomas Jefferson were expert astrologers. The emblem shown is an Egyptian °pyramid in the apex of which appears the third °eye of °clairvoyance. *Annuit Coeptis*, the inscrip-

guide

29. Reverse of the Great Seal of the USA

tion under the upper circumference, means 'he prospers our undertaking', and that in the lower, *Novus Ordo Seclorum*, means 'new order of the ages', referring to the Gold, Silver, Bronze and Iron Ages which comprise 26,000 years. The Aquarian Age in astrological terms, into which we have advanced, is one-twelfth of this span, and symbolizes altruism, brotherhood and synthesis, as distinct from greed, separation and division; °ill. 29.

guide. Every human being has a °spirit guide, though most people are so insensitive that they are unable to contact their guides or benefit from their advice. The °psychics who can have developed the ability to call on their guides almost at will and seek advice and information. °Mediums are asked why their guides are Red Indian chiefs, Egyptians, Hindus, Chinese sages and wise men from past ages; the reason is that such men have experienced many °reincarnations and have mastered the lessons they were meant to learn while on earth, and in return have the power to benefit the living. They can, however, get in touch with normal people only through °mediums.

Guppy, Mrs Samuel (Agnes Nicols). A direct voice °medium discovered by Alfred Russel Wallace in 1861. She introduced the prototype of the darkened cabinet because in a limited, darkened space sufficient power was built up for the construction of a materialized figure able to stand scrutiny in the light. Her most fantastic claim was that on 3 June 1871 she was projected from her home in Highbury to Lamb's Conduit Street, several miles away. As she weighed over 200lb and the transportation took place without observers, her account of this event has been regarded sceptically.

Gurdjieff, Georges Ivanovitch (1867–1949). Born in Georgia, USSR, within sight of Mt Ararat. Though some say he could trace his lineage back to the Greeks of Caesarea, he was in all probability an Armenian carpet-dealer, who amassed a considerable fortune, which enabled him to visit Tibet, Turkestan, Persia and other countries, possibly including India. An original thinker who taught a peculiar cosmic system at about the time of the Russian Revolution, he later visited the USA and finally settled in Fontainebleau, France, where he established the Institute for the Harmonious Development of Man. His system embodied dancing, close contact with nature, and concentrated on body control. He believed that most people are half-asleep all their lives and that his teachings would enable them to attain an advanced state. His semi-autobiographical work called *All and Everything*, which was completed shortly before his death, was iconoclastic. P. D. °Ouspensky was probably his greatest pupil. Students at his Institute were guests for 2 weeks at a time but had to do housework, gardening, wood chopping and other chores and to practise the 6,000 physical movements to music prescribed by him. Only in this way, he believed, could old habits and automatic functioning be broken down and the °astral body be born. In 1930 he had a car accident which forced him to close his Institute and devote himself to writing.

Gurney, Edmund, MB (1847–1887). Graduate of Trinity College, Cambridge; a member of the well-known banking family. He studied at University College Medical School and entered St George's Hospital but, as he could not abide the sounds and sights there, he read for the bar. He was also a keen musician and in 1880 wrote *The Power of Sound*, *Tertium Quid* (essays) and philosophical papers for *Mind*. Became Hon. Secretary of the °Society for Psychical Research in 1883, where he did valuable work on °hypnotism. He was the main author of *Phantasms of Living*, a work describing 702 cases, which made a tremendous impact. His early death was perhaps the greatest single blow to psychical research.

guru. Spiritual teacher; the word comes from the Sanskrit *gur* (to raise, to uplift). *Gurudeva* is a divine person or spiritual preceptor, and *param-guru* is a supreme guru or guru beyond; a consultant and a colleague; a °guide; but not an instructor or a dictator. The guru indicates the path along which his *chela* or follower must tread, but he will not insist or force him to do so.

H

hallucination. Sense perception without relevant or adequate sensory stimulation. Failure to have perceptual experience when relevant and adequate stimuli are present is sometimes called negative hallucination, and both types are produced by °hypnosis. Phenomenon thought to be produced by abnormal or pathological mental conditions, but which is quite frequent between sleep and waking, or just before falling asleep or just before waking.

hallucinosis. Disordered mental condition; subject to the occurrence of °hallucinations, without any necessary impairment of consciousness.

healing by touch. Healing by the laying-on of hands or touch is often referred to as °faith healing, but this is not accurate as faith is not a necessary ingredient. There is a flow of power from the healer to the ailing person, sometimes so vivid that a warm glow is felt. The most famous healer of this kind in the past was the Irishman, °Greatrakes, who in the 17th century was famous for the miracles he performed; °Carrel; °Chapman; George °Fox; °king's evil.

herbal medicine. The earliest remedies were simples, used after observation on animals. Illness was cured by eating herbs and broken limbs by being steeped in running water. When Man became civilized (6000–3000 BC), herbs were linked with the planets and there were different herbs for different types of people and different illnesses. There is a herb for every need: for destroying insects (e.g. rue); for attracting customers into a shop (basil); love charms (artemesias is known as Maiden's Ruin), etc. Doctors were versed in °astrology and prescriptions had an R in one corner, an invocation calling on Jupiter to use his power to effect a cure. In the 17th century William Cole advised that herbs should be gathered at the full moon as they were then richest in juice. Culpepper said that 'the admirable harmony of the Creation could be seen in the influence of the stars upon herbs and the body of Man'. Afflicted persons fought disease by using herbs of the plant that caused the disease, thus depression (Saturn) was fought with a stimulant (Mars). According to °astrology,

Aries and the first house rule stimulants; Taurus and the second house, mints; Gemini and the third house, parsley; Cancer and the fourth house, broccoli, cauliflower, sprouts, etc.; Leo and the fifth house, rosehips, tomatoes, angelica, anis and carroway; Virgo and the sixth house, all the teas; Libra and the seventh house, the thymes; Scorpio and the eighth house, cathartic foods, spinach, rhubarb and dandelion; Sagittarius and the ninth house, borage and marjoram; Capricorn and the tenth house, aconite, barley, beets and buckthorn; Aquarius and the eleventh house, bay leaves; Pisces and the twelfth house, mushrooms, toadstools, °mandrake, datura and opiate herbs. This does not mean that only people born under these signs will benefit from such herbs, but that diseases under such signs can best be cured by them; °Steiner.

Hodgson, Richard (1855–1905). Brilliant Australian lawyer who came under °Sidgwick's influence at Cambridge. In 1884 went to India to investigate °Blavatsky. One of the first members of the °Society for Psychical Research, with a flair for unmasking fraudulent °mediums. In 1887 went to America where he took over the management of the °American Society for Psychical Research, collaborated in psychical research with °James and wrote widely on the subject.

Home, Daniel Dunglas (1833–1886). Born near Edinburgh, he spent the early part of his life in America, travelled in Europe, married Sacha de Kroll, daughter of a Russian general, and achieved fame as the greatest °medium of his time. He produced °apports from the air, made heavy furniture rise without human agency, and reputable witnesses testified that he levitated. *Experiences in Spiritualism*, written by Viscount Adare, contains an account of 78 seances between 1867–1869, and the Earl of Dunraven' said in the foreword, 'The manifestations were so remarkable that they deserve to be duly chronicled and preserved . . .' In 1871 °Crookes examined Home and published an account of the °psychic phenomena but, despite °Crooke's undoubted reputation, the Royal Society refused to read his report. Twenty years later, when °Crookes was elected President of the British Association for the Advancement of Science, he wrote, 'I find nothing to detract or alter. I have discovered no flaw in the experiments then made, or in the reasoning I based on them.' Dr Hare, Dr Paul, Dr M. Vest, and other eminent men recorded their belief in Home's integrity and gave evidence on his behalf and, though witnesses stated that he levitated his body, handled fire without getting burnt, and flew in and out of the third storey windows of a house, the

Hone

Society turned a deaf ear. Home died of tuberculosis in France; °levitation.

Hone, Margaret (1892–1969). President of the Society of British Astrologers, author of *Applied Astrology*, *Modern Textbook of Astrology* and other works; °astrology; °ill. 30.

30. Margaret Hone

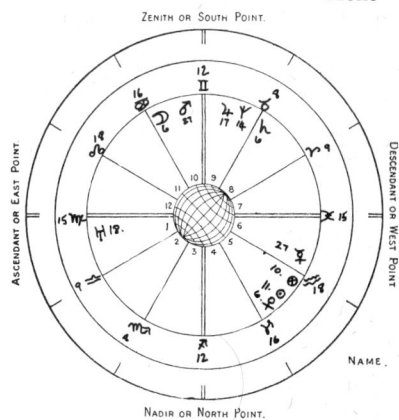

31. Horoscope of Franklin D. Roosevelt, born 30.1.1882 at 8pm in Poughkeepsie, USA

horoscope. An observation of the sky and the configuration of the planets at the instant of a person's birth. From this, and from the latitude and longitude of his birthplace, a plan of the 12 signs of the zodiac and the 12 houses in which they were at that moment is drawn up, from which his character and abilities can be seen and his future progress shown; °astrology; °ill. 31.

Huna. A psycho-religious system, the origins of which have been lost; probably an offshoot of °yoga or Berber °magic, or a mixture of both. Has been practised in Hawaii and Polynesia for centuries but suppressed when missionaries gained power and control. They denounced it as °black magic, made it illegal and, though practised in secret by a few, it almost died out. Eventually an American anthropologist, Max Freedom Long, investigated the cult which had been preserved by °kahunas (keepers of the secret). In 1848 he published *The Secret Science*

Behind The Miracles and the Huna Research Association was formed. Huna teaches that Man is a threefold being, consisting of the °unconscious, conscious and °superconscious, and the initial step is to train the °unconscious or lower self in order that it may co-operate with the middle and higher selves. To make prayer or °meditation effective, *mana* or the vital force must be sent along the *aka* (cord) to the higher self in the same way as the power of kundalini is released in °yoga. The ethics are much the same as those of all great religions, but the powers developed are astounding, e.g. their ability to summon sharks, speak to them and enter the water with them without being molested; it is this that saves so many islanders when they are shipwrecked.

Hurkos, Peter. The name by which newspapers call Peter Van Der Hurk, a Dutchman with no spiritualistic beliefs, who has baffled the world by accidentally developed °psychic powers. In 1943, when he and his father were painting a school, he fell from the top of a ladder and did not regain consciousness for 3 days. While in hospital with a fractured skull, he heard himself say to a patient in the next bed, 'You are a bad man'. When the patient, a grocer, asked what he meant, Hurkos told him that his father, who had died recently, had left him a gold watch, 'And you have sold it,' he said, which was true. Hurkos has collaborated frequently with the US police to trace murderers. He was in Britain when the Stone of Scone was removed from Westminster Abbey and told the police that it would be recovered in 3 weeks. It was.

hydromancy. Divination by the °colour, ebb and flow of water, from ripples produced by dropping pebbles into a pool – odd numbers being good, even numbers bad. Tea leaf and coffee ground readings developed from this.

hypnology. Scientific investigation of sleep, used by such pioneers of °hypnotism as Dr James Braid (1795–1860) for the study and practice of °hypnosis.

hypnopaedia. Learning or memorizing during sleep or semi-wakefulness due to hypnotic suggestion either by the human voice or from records and tapes; °hypnosis.

hypnosis. Derived from the Greek *hypnos* (sleep); *hypnoein* (to put to sleep); *hypnotikos* (drowsy, soporific). A condition resembling profound sleep, artificially induced, marked by °subconscious activity and sensitivity to suggestion. Hypnosis is not true sleep, in which blood drains gradually from the brain, causing brain anaemia, followed by loss of consciousness. During normal sleep it is impossible to perform some of the feats undertaken while under hypnosis, e.g. bear intolerable pain with impunity or recall incidents from the past which were forgotten. Dr Grey Walter says that, whereas anaesthetics produce regular and striking changes in brain rhythms and responses, hypnosis has no effect on them: 'Hypnosis shows none of the features of natural sleep; indeed, the more carefully we consider the subject's state, the less it seems to resemble anything we know of sleep. Awareness is not lost, but heightened – restricted, it is true, to certain categories of stimuli, usually the hypnotist's voice and suggestions. The significance of events is not reduced but absurdly emphasized – the power to learn is extended from its proper field of significant matter to any trifle the hypnotist may fancy'; °hypnotism.

hypnotherapy. The art of curing by inducing a state of °trance during which suggestions are placed in the mind of the patient to overcome the diseased condition.

hypnotic trance. Condition in which the subject is placed during °hypnosis.

hypnotism. The scientific study and practice of °hypnosis.

I

I Ching. °Yi King; °ill. 68.

imagination. The constructive, though not necessarily creative, employment of perceptual experience, revived as images in the form of ideas, but not necessarily a reproduction of past experience; often the sum total of material derived from past experience. It is either creative or imitative; creative when self-initiated and self-organized; imitative when following a construction initiated and organized by another.

incarnation. The state of being clothed in flesh or reality. This is our ultimate desire. First we perceive something that we wish to own or to happen, then we enjoy it, and, finally, it is completely attained and one arrives at a point of satiety, when the thing hankered after is no longer desirable. When the ideas and desires of the lower mind are rejected one can, by °meditation, incarnate oneself with the infinite; °reincarnation.

incubus. A feigned evil spirit or °daemon supposed to descend on persons in their sleep and especially to seek carnal intercourse with women. In the Middle Ages the

Indra Devi

existence of incubi was recognized by law; °succubus.

Indra Devi. Eugenie Petersen, half-Russian, half-Swedish, born before the First World War. Fascinated by °mysticism and oriental philosophy, she gravitated to India, endorsed the Freedom Movement and married a foreign diplomat. She became gravely ill with an 'incurable' heart complaint for 4 years, but was restored to health in 1 week by °yoga healing. This made her embrace °yoga and adopt the name Indra Devi. On the advice of her °guru she opened her first °yoga school in Shanghai and kept it going throughout the Japanese occupation. She returned to India and, in 1947, opened a °yoga school in Los Angeles, USA. Later introduced °yoga to Russia and lectured to a group including members of the Praesidium. Established an international °yoga centre in Tecate, Baja, California. Author of *Forever Young and Healthy*, *Yoga For Me* and *Renew Your Life Through Yoga*; °ill. 32.

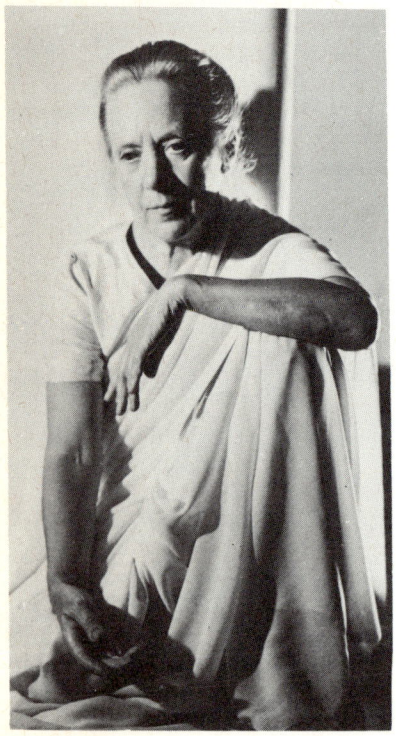

32. Indra Devi

influenced writing. Advice, guidance or °prophecy written under the influence of one who has passed over and is often the source of creative writing. In °automatic writing the words taken down may or may not make sense, but in influenced writing they are inspired. George Bernard Shaw said, 'When I write a play I do not foresee or intend a page of it from one end to the other; the play writes itself.' J.M. Barrie said his work was influenced by some force beyond his control; Charles Dickens that his 'brownies' wrote his novels; Socrates and Saint-Saens had °daemons who told them what to write, and Geraldine °Cummins, who was a famous °medium, wrote *The Scripts of Cleophas* and *They Survive* under the influence of her

°guide. Many others – Thackeray, Somerville, George Eliot, Kipling and Galsworthy – claimed to have been similarly influenced.

inspiration. A special immediate action or influence on the human mind; idea or purpose which prompts the creation of some work, design, painting, musical composition, invention or prophetic utterance. The prophets are said to be divinely inspired and the Bible written under divine influence. The muses of the Greeks were 9 sub-divisions of the higher emotions of the human mind, each providing a particular kind of inspiration.

intuition. Derived from the Latin *intuitio* (to look into) and philosophically it is the apprehension of an object by the mind without the intervention of any reasoning process. In °yoga it means °soul guidance, appearing naturally when the mind is calm and capable of receiving impressions. Intuitions are also received by °mediums and other sensitives whose minds are tuned in to receive °vibrations and waves of a frequency which make no impression on normal people. For those who have not reached this stage, emotions tend to control actions and the substance of the lower mind directs the emotions. Concentration and °meditation free the mind and make it receptive or intuitive to vibrations. °Telepathy and °dreams are not forms of intuition, because we have no control over them. During deep meditation the 'spiritual eye', situated in the centre of the forehead (the pineal gland), is able to 'see'. Intuition is a 'sixth sense' and one way in which it can be developed is by yoga.

J

James, Prof. William (1842–1910). Brother of Henry James, the writer, he delivered a lecture entitled 'The Energies of Men' to the Philosophical Association at Columbia University, USA, in 1909 in which he stated that a close friend, who had been chronically depressed, fatigued and broken in health, had taken up °yoga. After some months of *asanas*, breathing, concentration, °meditation and fasting, he aroused deeper levels of will and moral and intellectual power, and was free from a serious brain condition of the 'circular' type which had afflicted him for years. His entire mental and physical outlook changed for the better. James and Carl Lange, a Danish physiologist, propounded simultaneously a theory called the James–Lange Theory of Emotion, which explains emotion as the conscious experience due to the organic sensations that are aroused when the body is stirred by some powerful stimulus. James, who was a leader of the American °Society for Psychical Research, investigated °yoga.

Jaquin, Noel (1893–1974). Disciple of °Benham and the most famous British palmist in the 1930s. The first man in the West to try to place °palmistry on a scientific footing and divorce it from any suggestion of hocus-pocus, °magic or °clairvoyance. He studied not only the lines, but also the shape, texture, °colour and feel of hands, and the whorls on the fingers. From these he diagnosed the character of the subject, his tendencies and talents. He was the first palmist in Europe to diagnose disease from the hand. He also collaborated with Scotland

33. Noel Jaquin

Yard in assessing criminal tendencies in hands. His numerous books on the subject are regarded as standard works by students: *The Hand Of Man, The Human Hand, The Hand Speaks, The Signature of Time,* etc.; °ill. 33.

Johnson, Douglas. Famous for his °psychic powers which he has demonstrated on television in Britain and America. His power was first evident at the age of 6 when he said, 'Granny is coming to lunch', which his parents dismissed as childish fantasy. But Granny arrived, and ever since he has baffled audiences by his °second sight. Currently spends much of his time in the USA, where he gives private sittings in °clairvoyance and °psychometry. Has collaborated in experiments with Dr W.J. Roll at the University of Carolina and with °Garrett.

Judge, William Quan. Was appointed by Helena °Blavatsky as her representative in the USA. One of the founders of the °Theosophical Society and a True Master. In 1895, 4 years after °Blavatsky's death, he became President of the °American Society for Psychical Research. He founded the monthly magazines *The Path* and *The Theosophical Forum*. His *Ocean of Theosophy* is one of the most important books in the Society's literature.

ju-ju. Ritual connected with °charms, °amulets or any objects venerated by African tribes if these are supposed to possess supernatural powers; a ban or interdiction affected by such objects. Though in the past the power projected by ju-jus was ridiculed in the West, anthropologists and other investigators are now convinced that forces can be projected by impinging the mind of the °witch doctor on ju-jus and transferring the power of evil or good to a third person. Whether this is achieved by °hypnotism or by some force about which we know nothing is not certain.

Jung, Dr Carl (1875–1961). Was born at Kasswil in Thurgau, studied medicine at Basle, Zurich and Paris, and was a professor at the universities of Zurich and Basle. Worked with Sigmund °Freud for about 10 years, but eventually rejected the Freudian system and advanced the idea that there are, in addition to °unconscious repressed elements, elements common to all individuals which have never been conscious, and which constitute the general and collective unconsciousness of the human race. For years he investigated the symbols that arise in °dreams and daydreams, in insanity, in mystical and alchemical literature, and the myths and rituals of primitive peoples. When he attended the Indian Science Congress in 1937 in Calcutta, he said, 'When a religious method recommends itself as "scientific", it can be certain of its public in the West. °Yoga fulfils this expectation.' He meditated on °psi for 20 years and based his argument in *Naturerklärung und Psyche* on its existence. He also studied °astrology and, though he said that he could not prove it to be true, he admitted that it worked. About those concerned with the Arts, he said, 'They have not yet learned to be objective with their own psyche, to distinguish between the thing that you do and the thing that happens to you. We must learn to listen to what the psyche spontaneously says to us – through the °dream, through the work of art.'

K

Kabalah. Cabala, Quabalah. The Jews have 3 grades of knowledge: 1. the Pentateuch (5 books), inspired by God and written down by Moses, which all members of the faith are supposed to master; 2. the Talmud, studied mainly by priests and rabbis; 3. the Kabalah or esoteric knowledge imparted to initiates only, revealed mainly in a codified form which can be understood only after much study and research. This includes the Tanak (Old Testament). The Kabalah includes °occult knowledge and in medieval times greatly influenced Jewish, Christian and Muslim scholars, theologians and magicians, for it comprises a comprehensive system of symbolism, °angelology, daemonology and °magic, with sections on °reincarnation and messianism. It contains the entire body of Christian theology. Many Christians have been converted to Judaism after studying the Kabalah, though some eminent Jews, e.g. Moses Maimonides (1139–1205), one of their most famous physicians, have rejected it. Kabalists maintain that as every word, letter and point in the Kabalah has some significance, it cannot be translated, abbreviated or simplified. Though there are numerous commentaries on the Kabalah, few have mastered it. It was handed down by word of mouth to the rabbis of the Mishnah and the Talmud and is a mystical interpretation of the Tanak. Though there have been learned kabalists throughout the ages, few in modern times have probed its secrets with success. One such was Rabbi Shlomo el-Ymanani el-Harfi of the Bukharian quarter of Jerusalem, who lived before the Second World War. By treating the Scriptures as a series of coded messages and decoding them by working out the permutations and combinations of the letters, he was able to inform Jews whether relatives living in Germany were alive and well or were in concentration camps. At times he collaborated with the Palestine Police to solve some of their problems, for he maintained that the Kabalah is a practical instrument for the guidance of men and that those who unravelled its mysteries would find a plan for living.

Kabir. A Muslim mystic who lived in the 15th and 16th centuries and was a contemporary of °Nanak, founder of the Sikh religion. He abandoned Islam and, while retaining strict monotheism and a strong dislike of the caste system, he founded a religion constricted neither by dogma, scripture nor social framework. He tried to build a bridge between Hindus and Muslims, but failed because of the intractability of the Muslims. Like Gandhi, he practised °yoga.

kahunas. Priesthood of the °Hunas. It is believed that they have all died, taking their secrets with them.

kalelose gun. A °ju-ju used by °witch-doctors. It is shaped like a gun with an ivory barrel. °Magic powder is placed in the barrel and the gun is pointed in the direction of the victim. When lit, the powder ignites in a flash and, though there is no bullet, it is said to kill at a range of 5 miles or more. The existence of such guns was confirmed in an article in the *Central African Journal of Medicine* (November 1960) by Dr K.H. Lephene of Mulobezi Hospital, Northern Rhodesia.

kama. Desire or emotion. A term used by Hindus, Buddhists and °yogis; should not be confused with °karma. Kama is the memory of experiences, pleasant and unpleasant, good and bad, which generates emotions. This can sometimes develop or destroy and can be an obstacle to progress. By the use of intelligence and will-power good memories can be used and constructive habits formed which will further development. In this sense, emotions are not part of oneself but are the result of experiences. Desire or emotion should not be crushed or sublimated, but selected, purified and strengthened; °Buddhism; °yoga.

karma. The law of cause and effect. Every action, good or bad, has a positive reaction. According to the *Upanishads*, deeds and emotions are determined by past actions and habits, and there is no such thing as chance. Every action leaves a trace in the organism and determines future progress or the lack of it. Man can no more get rid of his karma than his shadow on a sunny day. If he strives to do what conscience tells him is right, his mind and °spirit develop and he gradually rises to a higher stratum. Good is invariably repaid by good and evil by retribution, though cynics point out that this does not appear to be so in a world where the wicked flourish. The °yogis believe that in subsequent °reincarnations rewards and punishments will be dealt out and that ultimately we experience every kind of existence. Through this fire of experience the spirit is tempered and eventually combines with the Supreme Entity. Rebirth is accepted by many religions though not perhaps in the same way. Karma is not °fatalism. Every man is his own judge and jury; his actions gain rewards and punishments. Karma that is bearing fruit cannot be annulled or abolished, but karma that is being built up by good deeds and kindness can modify or cancel evil in the past. Like most good ideas, that of karma has become corrupted. In Buddhist countries some people build pagodas to atone for sins or to store up virtue for the future, but such material offerings are not acceptable. Wealth alone, or benefits bestowed on the less fortunate, cannot wipe out evil karmas. We live in an age when money counts, but it will make no difference to our karmas. We shall reap exactly what we sow.

Kelts. Celts; an ancient people whom Plutarch says originated in the Crimea, spread their influence and culture throughout Northern Europe and survived finally in Brittany, Cornwall, Wales, the Isle of Man, Ireland and Scotland. Their languages have survived in Gaelic, Manx, Welsh and Cornish (now virtually extinct), and much of their culture is preserved in Ireland and in Wales. Their scholars were °Druids, a class which produced priests, chieftains, judges, teachers, astrologers and °magicians. After the Roman conquest, druidism lay dormant for centuries and the cult was linked with °superstition. There has been a distinct revival, however, during the last century which seems to strengthen each year.

Kilner, Dr Walter J., BA, MD, MRCP (1847–1920). While at St Thomas's Hospital, he wrote *The Human Aura*, in which he said that in the future the °aura would be photographed. The following year he devised his dicyanin screen consisting of 2 plates of glass $\frac{1}{8}$ inch apart, the space being filled with an alcoholic solution of dicyanin, through which the human °aura became visible. The first subject, a woman of 23, had a blue-grey °aura with rays emanating from her body. Kilner said that auric emanations were divided into 3 parts: outer °aura, inner °aura and °etheric double. The latter was a narrow black band or void $\frac{1}{8}-\frac{1}{16}$ inch from the body. Adjacent was the inner °aura extending about 5 inches, then the outer °aura, ovoid in shape, widest at the waist and tapering towards the legs. On average the outer °aura extended about 8 inches from the inner °aura. As a result of this and other experiments Kilner wrote *The Human Atmosphere*, published in 1921, and no other work on the subject appeared till *The Origin and Properties of The Human Aura* by Oscar Bagnall in 1937. Bagnall used pinacynol and methalene blue in his screen, and spectacles instead of dicyanin.

King, William (1890–?). An Irish medium born with the ability to see, read and interpret the human °aura, and to see into patients' minds. He discovered his gift very early. Though he had a large clientele of rich businessmen, he always helped anyone in need. As he was extremely sensitive, he never saw more than two clients a day, because he had to rid himself of one visitor's °aura before he could turn his attention to the next. Even a foggy day in London used to upset him for a week and nullify his powers, as did alcohol and heavy meals. His work is dealt with in *William King's Profession* by Charles Drage.

king's evil. During the reign of Edward the Confessor a young woman dreamed that if the King touched a painful tumour in her neck she would be cured. So she approached the King, knelt and begged him to touch her neck. He called for a bowl of water, dipped his fingers in it and placed them on her neck and after a few minutes the tumour burst and the poisons drained away. Since then various kings of England and France have cured scrofula – tuberculosis of the bones and lymphatic glands – by touch. Edward III used to give ailing people a gold coin, known as a touch piece, stamped on one side with the figure of St Michael and on the other with a three-masted ship. Charles I is said to have cured 100 patients on Midsummer Day 1633 in the Royal Chapel, Holyrood and Charles II more than 100,000. In 1684 the throng that clamoured to be touched was so great that several were trampled to death. William III discontinued what he called 'a papist custom' and under the Hanoverians the custom of curing the king's evil by touch was abolished; °healing by touch.

Kirlian, Semyon and Valentina. In 1935, while making adjustments to equipment they had designed, these two Russian scientists discovered that they could detect, without lens or camera, °auras thrown off by objects. These auras are invisible to the human eye and similar to those shown by °Kilner who, 50 years ago, predicted that auras would eventually be of value in medical diagnosis. The Kirlians placed 2 identical leaves, handed to them by a botanist, between the plates of their apparatus: in one a picture of energy flared up, in the other the light was feeble. The first leaf was healthy; the other was diseased. They made hundreds of experiments and after 30 years were given a research grant by a sceptical Ministry of Public Health. They found they could predict not only disease in humans and plants from auras, but also the onset of disease, for which pre-diagnosis they coined the word 'predictinosis'. About 3 years later the Americans, who had branded °Reich as a charlatan for his discovery of life energy in plants which he called *orgone*, took up similar research. Prof. Thelma Moss of the University of California, who exhibited interest in the subject, was invited to Russia where she was shown that Kirlian photography revealed characteristic colours significant in medical diagnosis. The scientist Ademko and his colleagues then proved that bio-plasma changes when placed in a magnetic field and is concentrated at points in the body which correspond to the 700 acupuncture points discovered by the Chinese thousands of years ago.

kobold. In German folklore a familiar °spirit haunting houses and occasionally helping the inmates; an underground °spirit haunting mines; a °gnome.

Krishnamurti, J. (1895–   ). He and his brother, Nilyana, who lived at Adyar, Madras, were noticed by °Leadbeater because of their unusual °auras. He obtained their father's permission to give them schooling and train them. Krishnamurti is now famous as a great teacher and an °avatara. He relinquished the house and possessions that had been given him, and advocates complete freedom and peace with oneself and society. He teaches that possessions enslave one and that self-imposed discipline should be cultivated. Has millions of followers. The basis of Krishnamurti's teaching is also that of °yoga: one should teach oneself to think clearly; one should always act in concert with nature and show compassion for all forms of life. He rejects such titles as teacher, prophet, preacher and °guru as these might stamp him as favouring some religion or society. He owns nothing and lives for mankind. His books include *Commentaries on Living*, *First and Last Freedom*, *Life Ahead*, *This Matter of Culture* and *Krishnamurti's Talks*; °ill. 34.

kung an. Tablets of truth. A method of °prediction with white pebbles polished to crystal smoothness and housed in a black velvet bag, the

34. J. Krishnamurti as a young man

mouth of which is small and tied with drawstrings. The whiteness of the pebbles is symbolic of the mind of the reader as he gazes at the stones; the colour of the bag reminds him of the 'bitter night of birth, death, illusion and deception from the depths of which all truth emerges'. The small opening is meant to remind him to be wary and not to make rash interpretations and °predictions. The pebbles are spread with a small white stick known as a *hua taw*. The reader counts them in groups of four and returns them to the bag. One, two or three may remain and it is from these that the reading is given. One signifies that the reading will be about the client's concern with things; two, with people; three, with self. If none remain the pebbles are cast again and divided into groups of five and a fresh start made.

L

Leadbeater, Rev. Charles Webster (1847–1934). Took orders in the Church of England as High Churchman and was appointed curate at Liphook, Hampshire, England. A long-standing interest in the °occult and in °spiritualism led to his introduction to °theosophy. He met °Blavatsky several times and joined the °Theosophical Society in 1884. Later he renounced his living and went to India, where his °psychic faculties were developed and he undertook a variety of clairvoyant investigations in England, India, Ceylon, America and Australia.

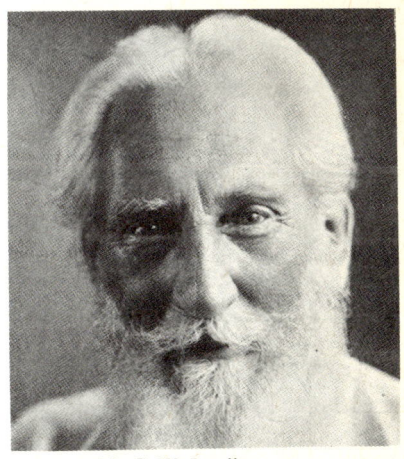

35. C. W. Leadbeater

Leaf

While in Adyar, Madras, he noticed that 2 children, °Krishnamurti and his brother Nilyana, had remarkable °auras, so obtained permission from their father to train them. In 1916 he helped to found the Liberal Catholic Church and became its Presiding Bishop. His clairvoyant studies included investigations into the hidden side of ceremonials in the Church and into Freemasonry, in which he also held exalted rank. His books include *The Chakras*, *Clairvoyance*, *The Science of The Sacraments*, *The Hidden Life of Freemasonry* and *A Textbook of Theosophy*. He died in Perth, Australia; °clairvoyance; °ill. 35.

Leaf, Horace (?–1971). Medium, author and lecturer. Originally a sceptic, his interest in the °occult was aroused when, while reading medicine at the University of London, a palmist told him of a number of 'impossible' events which eventually came to pass. While in Nashville, Tennessee, he discovered, quite by accident, that he possessed °second sight and was also a °medium. He then started lecturing and writing on the °occult, and practised with immense success as a °medium. One of the most widely travelled of °mediums, he enjoyed a fine reputation for integrity, especially among the business community in the USA.

Leaf, Walter (?–1971). Son of a wealthy British merchant banker and one of the early members of the °Society for Psychical Research.

Lee penny. Most famous of all Scottish °amulets, owned originally by an emir in the Holy Land, it was brought back to Scotland by Sir Simon Locard of Lee in about 1330.

36. Lee penny

It is a small, triangular stone, dull, opaque and raspberry in colour, set in a silver coin which hangs from a fine 6-inch long silver chain. It is supposed to avert misfortune and, when dipped in water, to act as a styptic and a febrifuge. It is now owned by Simon Macdonal Lockhart of Lee who lives in Dolphinton, Scotland; °ill. 35.

Leo, Alan (1860–1917). Son of a Scots soldier, he believed he was a °reincarnation and was one of the leading astrologers of his time. He started astrological work in 1880 and with Aphorel (F.W. Lacey) he founded *The Astrologer's Magazine*, which was renamed *Modern Astrology* in 1895. Leo wrote a number of important books, including *Astrology For All*, *Casting The Horoscope*, *The Art of Synthesis*, *Esoteric Astrology* and *How To Judge a Nativity*; °astrology; °horoscope.

Leonard, Gladys Osborne (1882–1968). Was first aware of her °psychic powers when she attended a spiritualist meeting. She was one of the few °mediums investigated by the °Society for Psychical Research who was found to be genuine. She was tested by °Lodge, Prof. E.R. Dodds and the Rev. C.R. Drayton Thomas. °Lodge said, 'She is the best, or one of the best, I have known.' She gave many convincing proofs of survival and on one occasion she told the War Office of the death of an airman, shot down in 1914, of whom they had no news. Later news came through that he was killed in exactly the same place and time seen by her; °clairvoyance; °spiritualism.

leopard men. The °witch-doctors of some African tribes have the ability to turn themselves into beasts and then back again into humans. Dr Gerald Kirkland, a Medical Officer and Deputy Sheriff in the African Colonial Service, is one of the many Europeans who have seen this phenomenon. Disguised as an African and hiding in a tree, he witnessed a ritual dance in which a man and a woman were transformed instantly into male and female jackals. Dr Frederick, a Government Medical Officer, also testified that he had seen a similar dance performed by the Nyanga, during which a man and a woman were suddenly turned into jackals. Sometimes the transformation is into a leopard or an immensely large reptile. Unfortunately such demonstrations are never made wittingly in the presence of Europeans and have not, therefore, been investigated by scientists.

leprechauns. In Irish folklore, a diminutive sprite. Belief in their existence is widely held in Ireland, where they are called 'the little people'. In remote parts of the country candles are lit and placed in windows so that leprechauns can see their way, milk and food are placed outside front doors, and for these gifts the little people render services. Recently a newly planned road had to be diverted because it would have destroyed a knoll inhabited by them, for officialdom apparently shares this belief and bowed to local feeling. To do anything to harm leprechauns is believed to bring bad luck.

Levi-Strauss, Dr Claude (1908–   ). Famous French anthropologist at the Ecole Pratique des Hautes Etudes in Paris, who exploded the idea that psychiatry is a discovery

levitation

of the 19th century. 'We overlook the fact,' he said, 'that psychoanalysis has simply rediscovered and expressed in new terms an approach to mental illness that goes back to the early days of mankind and which so-called primitive practitioners have always used, often with skill that amazes our foremost men of science.' He has written many books on anthropology and philosophy, and is a regular contributor to scientific journals.

levitation. The ability to lighten the body so that it defies gravity and rises into the air without being lifted or propelled. By this means one may traverse mountains, rivers and seas. Patanjali, the great °yogi, says that levitation can be achieved by mastery of the vital airs called *udana* and by learning *sanyama*. °David-Neel saw people being levitated during her travels in Tibet and °Cannon had personal experience of this phenomenon. °Home demonstrated levitation in Britain during the 19th century and °Twigg and others have seen demonstrations of levitation within recent years. It is not a new phenomenon – the Roman Catholic Church records that more than 200 saints have triumphed over the laws of gravity. When Ferdinand I was host to St Francis of Paula in Naples he saw a meditating monk floating high above the floor of his room, and St Teresa of Avila often rose, without assistance, to the ceiling. British officials in India have recorded instances of °yogis in the lotus pose floating on water or in the air. Today anyone who visits a mosque 50 miles south of Poona, India, dedicated to the °sufi saint Qumar Ali Dervish can witness an apparent miracle of levitation. If 11 people – no more, no less – bend and touch with their index fingers a boulder weighing 120lbs which rests outside the mosque and chant 'Qumar Ali Dervish!' in ringing tones, the boulder will rise 6 feet into the air, remain aloft for a moment and then fall. The theory is that °vibrations from the chant set in motion an electrical force, which travels through the people's bodies into the boulder, thus causing it to rise. If the number touching the boulder is increased, it will not move; °ill. 37

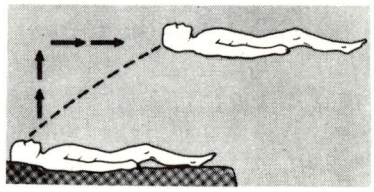

37. Levitation

Lilly, William (1602–1681). One of the great English astrologers, he was born in Diseworth, Leicestershire. In 1632 he began the study of °astrology and set up as a professional in 1641. The leading astrologers of the day attached themselves to political parties: Lilly was at first a Royalist but was so insulted by his colleagues that he went over to the Roundheads. His °predictions were so accurate that Cromwell patronized him, became his friend, and his fees made him wealthy. He is said to have predicted the Black Death, the Great Fire of London (1666) and the Restoration. At his death he left his autobiography to °Ashmole. In 1641 he compiled his most famous almanac, *Merlinus Anglicanus*, which was followed by other works of °prediction.

linga sharira. Subtle or psychical body; the Supreme Being, devoid of attributes or characteristic marks. It is the subtle body that contains the directives which give the °dense body its form and functions. It is the means by which we can see and hear at a great distance. This power, possessed only by highly developed °mediums, can project the subtle body. Some, however, in extremely bad health or near to death, suddenly have this ability.

Lodge, Sir Oliver (1851–1940). Principal of Birmingham University 1900–1920; President of the British Association for the Advancement of Science in 1913. His most important work was in the examination of the °ether and radio telegraphy. He wrote *Life and Matter*, *Man and The Universe*, *Relativity*,

38. Sir Oliver Lodge

and *Science and The Universe*. After the death of his son, Raymond, he wrote *Life and Death*, and *Why I Believe In Personal Immortality*. He was a confirmed sceptic when he joined the °Society for Psychical Research at the same time as °Hodgson but, after his son's death, he had sittings with °Leonard and °Piper which convinced him of the existence of life after death; °ill. 38.

Lord-Drake, Maud (1852–?). Born in Iowa, USA. Ranks among the great mediums who, according to tradition, are born with a veil over the face. She had a double veil which made her father reject her as a child of the °Devil. At the age of 6,

lotus

she was scalded, with second- and third-degree burns all over her body, and the doctors said she would die. Her bandaged hands grasped a pencil and wrote on a blank prescription: 'Get pine needles, brush with linseed oil, put between beet leaves and apply immediately.' Dr Edison Woodruff recognized the writing as that of a dead colleague, did as instructed, and the child recovered. While under the influence of °spirits she could speak in a dozen languages, describe forms and give names. Her father refused to have her educated as he feared the scandal if manifestations took place publicly. She could locate coal deposits by placing a hand on the ground and would say how deep they were. She was also capable of spirit surgery and cured many who were given up by surgeons and doctors. She held °seances privately and in public, and foretold the future with remarkable accuracy. When Frances Hodgson Burnett, the novelist, went to her in despair because her work would not sell she was told, 'I see you writing a very poignant book. It will sweep the world. It will be dramatized.' Burnett's next book was *Little Lord Fauntleroy*; °dowsing; °psychic surgery; °xenoglossia.

lotus. Water-lily of Egypt and the East, it was considered the source of life by the Ancients. The flower is sacred to the Hindus, and Brahma is said to have been born in the heart of one. In Ancient Egypt the seeds were ground and made into bread, and were sown by being wrapped in balls of clay and thrown into the Nile, a practice which gave rise to the saying, 'Cast thy bread upon the waters.' It is the flower of power, a favourite symbol with teachers of the °occult in the East, for it represents the cosmos and Man. The seed contains within itself a perfect miniature of the future plant symbolizing the fact that spiritual prototypes of all things exist in the immaterial world. The lotus has its roots in the mud, grows through water and spreads its flower into the air above. The root represents material life; the stalk passing through water represents existence in the °astral world; and the flower floating on the water and opening up to the sky is emblematic of spiritual being. In °yoga the lotuses or °chakras are the subtle focuses of consciousness; they are represented as lotuses of different colours to assist °meditation, the aim being to concentrate life force and nervous energy, and make these flow along the *shushumna* to the higher level of the brain by concentrating on the thousand-petalled lotus in that area.

lycanthropy. Power to transform oneself into a wolf; form of madness in which the patient imagines himself to be some beast and exhibits depraved appetites, changes of voice, etc.; °leopard men; °werwolves; °wolfmen.

M

Mackenzie, Kenneth. °Brahan Seer.
macumba. A form of °voodoo practised in Brazil. Though Brazil is a predominantly Roman Catholic country, Christianity and macumba co-exist, and many intellectuals have turned to macumba, which they find more exhilarating and satisfying than anything Christianity has to offer. It is a mixture of ritual Christianity and the Muslim and Jewish religions.
magic. The pretended art of influencing the course of events by compelling the agency of spiritual beings, or bringing into operation some °occult-controlling principle of nature; °sorcery; °witchcraft; working or produced by enchantment (OED). There are 2 kinds: °black magic, which involves the invocation of devils and evil spirits, and white magic, in which use is made of °charms, the repetition of powerful formulae, °vibrations, chanting and ritual. °Voodoo is a form of °black magic. °Ju-ju may be either °black or white, for there are °ju-ju men who work to protect, whereas others set out to destroy. °Astrology and °hypnotism were once considered to be forms of magic but are not so today. The achievement of certain aims is called magic when it is brought about by circumstances which contravene or are outside the boundaries of known scientific laws and the phenomenon produced baffles investigation, but this merely means that the forms used are unknown or have not been studied. °Astral projection, °clairvoyance, °ESP and °faith healing were all once considered within the orbit of magic and those who practised them were dubbed °witches. Today serious investigation is taking place into all forms of magic and attempts are being made to harness it in the fields of medicine and psychiatry.
magician. One skilled in °magic or the pretended art of influencing the course of events by compelling the agency of spiritual beings, or by bringing into operation some °occult-controlling principle of nature; sorcery; °witchcraft; anything that exceeds the bounds of human understanding at any time. Magicians' manuals were known as *grimoires* or Books of Power.
magnetism. °Animal magnetism.
magnetotherapy. A system of curing

Mahomet

disease invented by Dr Elisha Perkins (1741–1799) by touching living tissue with metals. Sometimes metals were used alone, at other times in combination, such as copper, zinc and a little gold, or iron, silver and a little platinum. He read a paper on his findings to the Connecticut Medical Society in 1795 but, though Elliotson, Luys and °Charcot, all eminent in their various fields, subsequently proved that metals and magnets influence the human body, magnetotherapy has fallen into disuse.

Mahomet, Mohammed, Mahummud (570–632). An inspired prophet and founder of Islam, who was an outstanding °medium. Though an orphan and penniless (he was the heir of a noble family), his talents and industry made him head of a trading firm owned by a wealthy widow whom he married. He refused, however, to consider her wealth as his own, as was the custom. He frequently retired to a cave on Mt Hira to meditate and there developed °clairaudience. One day a voice echoed in the cavern, commanding him, 'Read! Read!' and a third time, 'Read!' 'I cannot read,' he cried in despair, but the voice reiterated, 'Read! in the name of the Creator that formeth Man from a seed cell.' Then the book known as the *Koran* (*quran*: reading, recitation) was revealed to him. Only later was he to learn that his °spirit guide was Jibra'il (Gabriel) who 6 centuries earlier had revealed to the Virgin Mary the coming birth of the Prophet Issa (Jesus). Mahomet also developed other forms of mediumship such as °clairvoyance and he once interrupted a public sermon to announce the critical state of a battle taking place hundreds of miles away. He said that Jibra'il had materialized completely from the spiritual form from 'the foetus to the finger-tips' on his visits of instruction to Mahomet; °ill. 39.

Mahummud. °Mahomet.

mandrake. Any plant of the genus mandragora, often confused with °ginseng. Its forked root roughly resembles the human body, which probably accounts for its role as a

39. Part of the *Koran* (*British Museum, Crown Copyright*)

40. Engraving of a mandrake from John Gerrard's *The Grete Herball* (1529)

°magic plant; frequently used as an aphrodisiac in various countries. The plant was said to sweat blood and to shriek when uprooted. Those who heard this terrible sound either died or became insane; °ill. 40.

Manning, Matthew (1955–). Born near Cambridge, England. One of the most extraordinary of modern °psychics: he can bend spoons, forks and other metal objects more impressively than Uri Geller, but says: 'I don't like doing it because it is harnessing a destructive force', and refuses now to bend metal. Among the objects he has bent, however, are a pair of 'Clejuso' handcuffs, made in Western Germany of metal claimed to be unbendable and unbreakable, which are used by the Special Branch in Britain. He can also diagnose health through communicators and does °automatic writing and drawing. Matthew first became aware of his powers when he was 11 and his family lived in an 18th-century house. When on holiday from Oakham School, Rutland, the furniture in his bedroom started to move, and chairs and tables were upturned. When everything was replaced, he and his family went into the dining-room to find it in a state of total confusion. Furniture had been overturned and objects hurled about with great force. On his return to school, some of the 26 boys in his dormitory were tipped out of their two-tiered bunks and his own was shifted 18 inches. Because of these manifestations, the headmaster was twice on the point of asking his

41. Matthew Manning

parents to remove him. The disturbances ceased, however, when he channelled his energy into automatic writing, not only in English but in Old English, Latin, Russian and Arabic script, none of which were known to him. His father consulted Dr George Owen, a Cambridge mathematician and an authority on °poltergeists, and some years later Prof. Brian Josephson of the Cavendish Laboratory, who examined Matthew, said: 'I think we are on the verge of discoveries which may be extremely important in physics. We are dealing with a new kind of energy. This force must be subject to laws. I believe ordinary methods of scientific investigation will tell us a lot about psychic phenomena. They are mysterious but no more mysterious than a lot of things in physics today.' Manning also spent a fortnight in Freiburg, Germany, where °Bender carried out experiments with him; °ill. 41.

mantra. Word, syllable or phrase with sacred or spiritual associations which, repeated continuously, produces either beneficial or harmful °vibrations. The art was born in Ancient India to achieve specific ends, such as improved health, spiritual awareness, etc., and the best known of all mantras is OM. Vedic literature has been passed down through the centuries by word of mouth as nothing was written down. °Yogis have to memorize the 4 Vedas (Rig-Veda, Sama-Veda, Yajur-Veda and Athara-Veda) by heart – a tremendous feat – and pronounce the words exactly as they were originally pronounced. By doing so, they produce the right °vibrations, which endow them with what might be called supernatural power. Mantras have been developed in all forms by the great religions, and by black and white magicians, who call them incantations. The litanies, chanting and repetition of prayers in church, are mantras which help to concentrate the thoughts, increase spiritual awareness, develop breathing and improve health.

Marchocias. Being who is credited in °black °magic with having power; °Beelzebub.

materialization. The appearance of a °spirit in bodily form. The biologist allows Man one body, but the spiritualist admits the existence of two: the physical and the °etheric body. °Etheric matter is °ectoplasm and a materializing °medium is a person so constituted that his °ectoplasm can be drawn on to provide a temporary vehicle for some entity of the °astral world wishing to make contact with the physical world. An investigation into ectoplasm and materialism was conducted by W.J. Crawford, who described details in *The Reality of Psychic Phenomena.*

medicine men. Members of American Indian tribes who have inherited herbal lore, the study of the skies, the seasons and natural changes, and who have developed clairvoyant powers which give them a special place in the tribe. They are healers, have °visions and in the past their status was unchallenged. Recently the US Government has recognized them officially. In Africa the medicine man enjoys an even greater status as he is feared. He dabbles in °magic, casts spells, invokes °spirits and, if displeased, can harm. Primitive tribes in other parts of the world – South America and the Arctic – have medicine men too.

meditation. This is the essence of °yoga practice, without which knowledge of self cannot be acquired. It is the continuous mental effort to impinge the mind on a single object, idea or topic and cannot be put into practice without first mastering the art of concentration which, once mastered, becomes second nature and needs no effort. The aim is to discover the truth about ourselves, to think constructively and to open the gateway to true knowledge.

medium. Any intervening substance through which a force acts on objects at a distance or through which impressions are conveyed to the senses; a person supposed to be the organ of communication with departed °spirits.

Mesmer, Franciscus Antonius (1733–1815). Born in Iznang, Germany; educated at the Jesuit College, Dillingen. He grew more interested in science than theology, forsook the Church and enrolled in the medical school of the University of Vienna. Financially independent and able to experiment, he put many of his ideas into practice. He wrote a thesis entitled *De Platinarium Influx*, in which he explained that a mysterious fluid emanated from the stars, filling the universe, and, if a proper balance between this fluid and the body was not maintained, disease would result. He used to 'magnetize' bits of wood and glasses of water, and those who touched the wood or drank the water were cured of disease. We know that wood and water cannot be magnetized, but when Mesmer, robed impressively, walked among his patients and passed his hands over them, while soft music was played behind thick curtains, he hypnotized them. Mesmer also used suggestion to cure and said that a healing fluid emanated from his brain, nerves and will, which he called °animal magnetism. This we now know was hypnotic influence, but it was originally named °mesmerism after him. He was hounded by the medical profession, but the King of Prussia sent Wolfart, his personal physician, to study under him and the Swedish, Russian and Austrian governments sent their experts to learn his methods. He went to Paris, where Marie Antoinette became his patron. During the

Revolution he sought refuge in Switzerland, where he spent the remainder of his life treating the needy. Sometimes he stroked their aching limbs and sufferers from violent convulsions would pass into a deep sleep. He claimed that in his apartment called 'la salles des crises', the evil in the body was released and, on waking, patients found that their symptoms had vanished. Some patients had merely to sit in a chair over which he passed his hands to be either calmed or convulsed and there is no doubt that he possessed a tremendous ability to convey suggestion; °hypnosis; °hypnotism.

mesmerism. °Mesmer's 'animal magnetism', which we know now was hypnotic influence, was so-called after his name; °hypnotism.

metempsychosis. °Transmigration of the °soul of a human being or animal at death into a new body; °reincarnation.

middle eye. °Third eye.

middle way. °Buddhism.

mind. The organized totality of physical structures and processes, conscious, °unconscious and endopsychic; philosophically rather than psychologically, the entity of substratum underlying these structures and processes. Though the mind is a product of the brain and the generator of thought, it is conditioned by internal and external events and is linked to the physical and the spiritual body. The various levels of the mind are now recognized: conscious, °subconscious, °superconscious, and the °unconscious during sleep. There is much that we do not know about the mind and we cannot, for instance, say with certainty what happens when it is under the influence of °hypnosis, or during sleep or °astral projection.

mineral vibrations. Minerals produce °vibrations of varying frequencies that affect those who come into contact with them, either favourably or adversely depending on the planets under which the person is born: Aries, iron (organic); Taurus, copper; Gemini, mercury (used externally); Cancer, fluoride of lime; Leo, gold; Virgo, zinc (traces only); Libra, manganese; Scorpio, iron; Sagittarius, tin; Capricorn, lead; Aquarius, lodestone; Pisces, organic iodine.

miracle. A marvellous event exceeding the known powers of nature and, therefore, supposed to be due to special intervention of the deity or some supernatural agency; chiefly an act (e.g. of healing) exhibiting control over the laws of nature and serving as evidence that the agent is either divine or specially favoured by God. Any act, such as °levitation, that supervenes the known physical laws.

Mohammed. °Mahomet.

moles, °prediction by. Moles (small lumps on the human skin) are the result of the influences of the planets or of the rising sign at birth. Those under Saturn are black; Jupiter, purple-brown; Sun, yellow; Venus, light brown; Mercury, honey-coloured; Moon, bluish-white. They have been used for centuries to denote character, temperament and future events: e.g. a mole at the nape of the neck indicates danger of drowning; on the gullet, danger of strangulation; near the right shoulder, covetousness; on a woman, that she will be loved by a prince or someone of very high rank. Moles of one °colour on one part of the body have different meanings to moles of the same colour on other parts. As the entire body has to be examined to give a comprehensive reading, mole readers are comparatively rare; °astrology; °signs of zodiac.

moon. The moon has a powerful °occult influence for, though it has no light of its own and reflects light and power from the sun, it plays a significant part in the lives of people. The word 'lunatic' is derived from the Latin *luna* (moon), and those in charge of asylums for the insane know that inmates grow excessively boisterous when the moon is full. People in the tropics, where moonlight is far more intense than in Britain, are said to get moonstruck (a form of paralysis of the face) if they sleep in the open under a full moon, and certain fish become poisonous if the moon is allowed to play on them after being netted. Sleeping animals invariably move from strong moonlight into shade. Tides the world over rise and fall by the attraction of the moon, even the water in wells far inland rises and falls as the moon waxes and wanes (c.f.: *Calendar Evolution and Simplification*, Moses Cotsworth). Plants are also affected and their growth can be stimulated if crops are sown just before or just after full moon. The Ancients planted according to the moon and mated their flocks to coincide with its rising. Within the last 20 years scientists in the USA and Australia have proved that the moon affects rainfall, governs floods and drought. Some criminologists maintain that it may cause sleepwalking in some and drive others to violent acts. Till recently these researchers have remained silent for fear of ridicule, but for centuries °astrology has associated the moon with conception, fertility, human feelings, population and mass movements. In the °horoscope of a woman the moon represents her personality; in that of a man it points to the woman or women in his life who have influenced him. As the moon constantly changes, it denotes changes, emotions, enthusiasms, depression and elation; °ill. 42.

Moore, Dr Francis (Old Moore) (1656–1715). Born in Bridgnorth, Shropshire, on 29 January; settled in Lambeth, London, and at the

42. Two Bathurst Island aborigines taking part in the Purukupali (Moon Legend) Dance, a story of their home territory which lies off the coast from Darwin, Australia. In the timeless time, Tapana, the moon, stole Waiei, the wife of Purukupali while the latter was out hunting. In the absence of his parents, their baby son died of neglect. Tapana undertook to return the boy to life within three days, but Purukupali refused, saying that everybody must now die, as his son had. In an ensuing fight Tapana was defeated and returned to the sky, his wounds being visible still as the lunar seas and craters we can see with the naked eye. The griefstricken Purukupali drowned himself; Waiei turned into a curlew, and her sad cries can still be heard as she wanders the land searching for her dead child. The picture shows the fight between Purukupali and Tapana.

age of forty-two he produced his almanack. In it he undertook to cure diseases, and Lysons describes him as one of the most remarkable men of his time, for he was schoolmaster, physician and astrologer combined. The almanack, started in 1699 to advertise pills and potions, was called *Kalendarium Ecclesiasticum* and contained weather prophecies. The following year he issued *Vox Stellarium, Being An Almanack for*

1701, which contained astrological observations. After his death, Tycho Wing, Thomas Wright and Harry Andrews, a mathematician, carried on his work. The 'Almanack' had a circulation of 500,000 copies a year, every copy having the sanction of the Archbishop of Canterbury before it could be published. Andrews then had the printing rights transferred to Pearsons of Birmingham and thereafter it carried a column about the influence of the moon on the human body, and in the latter part of the 18th century it contained poetry.

Mormonism. Religion founded by Joseph °Smith.

Moses, Rev. Stainton (1839–1892). An Oxford graduate who, on being introduced to °spiritualism by friends, realized that he was a powerful °medium who could produce °psi phenomena and °automatic writing. He was one of the fathers of modern °spiritualism whose 'spirit teachings' have been reprinted scores of times and are to be found in most °occult libraries. At first he was a sceptic who doubted even the source of his own °automatic writings and it took years for him to be convinced. There is no doubt about his integrity, for he had nothing to gain and, in the 19th century, he had in fact a great deal to lose by his endorsement of °psychic phenomena; °ill. 43.

Murphy, Bridey. *The Search for*

43. Rev. Stainton Moses

Bridey Murphy was written by Morey Bernstein, a businessman from Pueblo, Colorado, USA, who took up °hypnotism as a hobby. He hypnotized Ruth Simmons, who was brought up by a Norwegian uncle and a German–Scots–Irish aunt, and took her back in time – an experiment in regression. Under °hypnosis she said she was born in Cork, Eire, in 1798, died in 1864 and was re-born in the USA in 1923. She gave numerous details of her former existence, some of which were found to be accurate and others not – many could not be checked. *Life* magazine asked the opinions of a number of scientists, among them Dr Jerome Schneck, former President of the Society for Clinical and Experimental Hypnosis, and Dr Lewis Wolberg, Medical Director

Myers

of the New York Post-Graduate Centre for Psychotherapy, who agreed that people under deep °hypnosis are abnormally suggestible, but that an adult in a hypnotic °trance might display uncanny inventiveness, talk in a foreign language he does not understand, or recite verbatim from a book that was read to him at the age of 3. Their verdict was neither completely for nor against the evidence.

Myers, Frederic (1843-1901). An inspector of schools who devoted much of his time to °psychic phenomena. One of the founder members of the °Society for Psychical Research. He belonged to the Sidgwick Group which subsidized the °SPR to the extent of £700 a year and later financed the American SPR till it was independent.

mystic. An exponent of mystical theology; one who seeks by contemplation and self-surrender to obtain union with, or absorption into, the Deity, or one who believes in the spiritual apprehension of truth inaccessible to the understanding; anchorites; °dervishes; °yogis.

mystical wheel of Pythagoras. Pythagoras, one of the greatest mathematicians of all time, founded a school or society, half-religious, half-philosophical, in which disciples underwent a comprehensive training in gymnastics, mathematics and music, practised vegetarianism and believed in immortality and the transmigration of souls. Among other things, he established the first principle of the universe in number and is regarded as the founder of geometry and the discoverer of the musical octave. The proof of the forty-seventh proposition of Euclid is attributed to him. 'The function of geometry,' he said, 'is to draw us away from the sensible and the

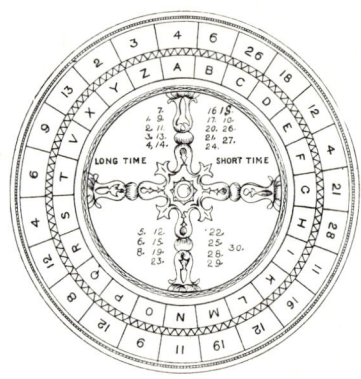

44. Wheel of Pythagoras, from a woodcut (1657)

perishable to the intelligent and the eternal, for the contemplation of the eternal is the end of philosophy, as the contemplation of the mysteries is the end of religion.' He adopted a religious attitude to mathematics, and the growth of religious mysticism based on mathematics is ascribed to his school. He invented the mystical wheel which resolves questions by a form of sortilegy by

mysticism

numbers, in which the result depends upon the unfettered agency of the mind and will, or the serious intent to know any difficult thing. Those who know how to work the wheel can resolve all questions on all matters whether of the past, present or future; °ill. 44.

mysticism. Belief in the attainment, through contemplation, of truths inaccessible to the understanding; sometimes used of philosophical theories assuming agencies of which a rational account cannot be given; °mystic.

N

Nanak (1469–1538). The founder of the Sikh religion; a strict monotheist and a determined opponent of caste. He gained his revelation from Heaven and organized the Sikhs into a close-knit, exclusive community of which he became the °guru. The fifth °guru, Arjun (1563–1606), collected the writings of Nanak and those who came after him, to compile the sacred book of the Sikhs called *Adi-Granth*, popularly known as °*Granth Sahib*, the Lord's Scripture. One of the rituals is to drink sweetened water from a communal bowl, which effectively destroys caste; °Kabir.

nature spirit. A °spirit supposed to reside in some element or object; °dryad; °faun; °gnome; °salamander; °sylph; °undine.

Naylor, John (1920–   ). One of R. H. °Naylor's 6 sons, he was educated at Marylebone and Bournemouth Grammar Schools, and London University. He studied °astrology under his father and set up in practice in 1949. After his father's death, he became a regular contributor to *Prediction* as well as the leading women's magazines and national newspapers. A weekly feature by him is syndicated

45. John Naylor

throughout the Commonwealth. He is President of the Federation of British Astrologers, author of works of fiction and publisher of numerous astrological annuals; °ill. 45.

Naylor, R.H. Though he left school at the age of 14, he attended night school, read widely and became a self-taught Latin scholar of distinction. He practised °astrology assiduously and went into partnership with °Cheiro (Count Louis Hamon), who founded the London Publishing Company. In 1925, when °astrology was associated in the minds of the public with hocus-pocus and °black magic, Naylor helped to place it on a scientific footing. In 1930 John Gordon of the *Sunday Express* commissioned him to do a feature on Princess Margaret, which brought such an overwhelming response that he was given a regular column. Of his many °predictions the most important were the R101 disaster and the gutting of the Crystal Palace by fire. The *Sunday Express* feature ended abruptly when during the last war he was accused of spreading alarm and despondency by predicting the fall of France and the invasion of Norway; but he also predicted the battle of Matapan and the battle of the River Plate. His features in *Prediction* did more than anything to establish that magazine and make it the success it is today.

necromancy. Art of predicting by means of communication with the dead; °magic.

nengraphy. °Thought photography; spirit photography.

nirvana. From the Sanskrit *nir-va* (to blow out). According to ancient lore, it means complete freedom; in Buddhist lore, liberation. The goal of the Buddhist is to achieve nirvana, a condition where there is neither earth nor water nor fire nor air; neither infinite space nor infinite consciousness; nor the sphere of void; nor the sphere of perception or non-perception. It is the end of woe; °Buddhism.

Nixon, Robert (1467–?). Known as the Cheshire Prophet, was born at Over, Winsford, England. The younger son of a husbandman. Robert, short, squat, with a great head and protruding eyes, was subnormal in intelligence, and was baited by other children. One day while ploughing, he stopped and remained still for more than an hour. Then, speaking in cultured tones, he prophesied on current affairs for more than 15 minutes. Thereafter, from time to time, he continued to make °prophecies concerning famous people and national events, all of which came true. Of William of Orange he said, 'The invading King shall be killed and laid on his horse's back like a calf' In 1702 William was thrown from his horse and his men laid him on his back and carried him to safety, but he died of his injuries. Nixon's most astonishing °prophecy, however, was 'Where carriages without horses go, then comes Old England's woe'. He said that this would take place in the reign of George II, which is when the steam engine was invented. He also prophesied that men would fly, that fire would rain down from the skies, and many other events that have since come to pass.

Nostradamus (1503–1566). A French astrologer of Jewish descent, who is still remembered for his prophecies. His real name was Michel de Notredame or Nostredame and he was born in Provence. At Avignon he studied philosophy and then read medicine at Montpellier. About 1547 he began to make his prophecies, publishing at Lyon in 1555 a book of rhymed prophecies entitled *Centuries*. Some of his prophecies seem to have been fulfilled and his fame became such that he was invited to visit Catherine of Medici. Charles IX appointed him his physician-in-ordinary; °astrology; °ill. 46.

46. Nostradamus

numerology. The art of predicting by numbers, which is based on the theory that every digit from one to nine produces °vibrations which affect the destinies of people. The fadic number or the °magic number of destiny is obtained by adding up all the digits in the date of birth, i.e. day, month and year. It matters not whether this is done vertically or horizontally, the result is always the same. The numbers, which are ruled by planets, are endowed with their characteristics and by translating the meanings of the digits, sometimes in combination with other digits, the character, potential, future fortune and a great deal of other information can be gleaned. Some people have lucky numbers and others unlucky ones; for instance, the number of a house can influence the fate of a resident and if he changes to a more fortunate number his luck will change. Each letter in the alphabet corresponds to a number and, therefore, names have numbers too, so that the changing of a name can bring a change of luck. The influence of numbers can be seen in the lives of many well-known men. W.K. Kellogg, pioneer of pre-cooked breakfast foods, was a seventh child, born on the seventh day of the week, on the seventh day of the seventh month; his father was a seventh child and the name Kellogg has 7 letters. Throughout his life he insisted on staying in rooms numbered 7 on the seventh floors of hotels and specified that his car numbers should always end in the number 7. As he became a multi-millionaire, there may be something in the theory! Gladstone's life was dominated by the number 5, Attlee's by 3, Lloyd George's by 9 and Churchill's by 1. Numbers have always possessed a special significance and mention of their power is made in the Bible, the °Kabalah and in various Hindu and other religious books.

nymph. One of a class of semi-divine beings, imagined as beautiful maidens inhabiting the seas, rivers, fountains, hills, woods, or trees, or attending on superior deities.

O

obsession. A persistent and recurring idea, usually strongly tinged with emotion, and frequently involving an urge towards some form of action, the whole mental situation being pathological. This may be produced by hypnotic influence or by some form of °magic such as that used by °witch-doctors and °ju-ju men, who from a distance can implant an idea in the mind of the victim and make him believe that he is evil, or an animal, or they can force him to commit a crime – even murder – or commit suicide. An obsessed person is completely in the power and under the control of someone else. Sometimes a °spirit, either good or bad, enters and takes possession of the body. There are several accounts in the New Testament of Jesus casting out devils who had taken possession of people. Dr Carl Wickland describes several cases in *Thirty Years Among The Dead*, and in 1926 Dr Mangin reported 2 remarkable cases to the Congress of Psychical Research in Copenhagen.

occult. Derived from the Latin *occulere*, meaning anything hidden or concealed; secret; communicated only to the initiated; recondite, mysterious; not apprehensible by the mind; is applied to sciences involving the knowledge or use of the supernatural, such as °alchemy, °astrology, °clairvoyance, °numerology, °palmistry and °theosophy. °Astrology and °palmistry do not come into the category of exact sciences for, though both are governed by laws, they take into consideration the influence of the planets, which has no proven scientific basis.

occultation. In °astrology, the disappearance of a star in the sun's rays when its apparent position is near that of the sun.

odic force. Baron Karl von Reichenbach (1788–1869), an eminent industrial chemist, carried out experiments with sensitive human subjects and found that they could feel a cold current near the north pole of a magnet, and distinguish a bluish flame or vapour in the dark. He found that substances – stones, rocks, °gems – produced similar phenomena. He called this discovery odic force in his *Researches on Magnetism, Electricity, Light, Crystallization and Chemical Attraction in Their Relation to Vital Force*, published in 1850. Dr M. Bircher-Benner called it chemical energy and thought it was a component of sunlight. Others have called it °ether, bio-cosmic energy, cosmic °orgone energy, and the °yogis call it *prana*, which they say is a constituent of the atmosphere.

Olcott, Colonel H.S. (1832–1907). Member of an old English Puritan family, born in New Jersey, USA. After a distinguished scholastic career, he became Professor of Agriculture at Athens, then founded

47. Col. H. S. Olcott

the Westchester Farm School and was a pioneer of national agricultural education. He fought for the North in the Civil War, attaining the rank of colonel in the Medical Corps. He was co-founder, with °Blavatsky, of the Theosophical Society, New York, which had an establishment in Adyar, India, and another in London; °ill. 47.

Old Moore's Almanack. The correct title is *Foulsham's Old Moore's Almanack*, because for many years the predictions have been worked out by a team of 4 astrologers commissioned by that publishing firm, which took over the copyright from the Stationers Company at the turn of the century. Ever since 1701 when Dr Francis °Moore, the founder, predicted that 'the Turk will be very severe against Christians and, what is worse, those professing Christianity will afflict one another', some astoundingly accurate predictions have appeared in the Almanack. As forecasts have to be worked out two years in advance of publication and as astrologers have to interpret the signs (just as doctors diagnose from symptoms), there is room for error. In August 1974, for instance, the threat of severe earthquakes was predicted in Turkey. The signs pointed to chaos and disruption – and Turkey falls in a notorious earthquake zone. These signs could easily have been interpreted as signs of war and it is this latitude in interpretation that sometimes leads astrologers astray. The Almanack sells 1¼ million copies in Britain each year, separate editions being published in America and Australasia.

omen. A phenomenon supposed to foreshadow a future event, the two having no causal connection.

oracle. Agency or °medium through which a god is supposed to speak. The oracle at Dodona, for instance, detected messages in the whispering of oaks. Greek oracles favoured the Amphictyonic System in which cities surrounding any oracle bound themselves not to destroy any city belonging to the league, not to cut any of them off from spring water, either in war or peace, and to war against any who violated these principles. They founded the Greek league system, fostered colonial development to spread Greek culture throughout the Mediterranean and were regarded as the voice of the highest wisdom. Delphi became the 'navel of the world' and Apollo was worshipped as the founder of Sicily; °Delphic oracle; °sibyl.

orgone. Energy akin to static electricity with healing powers; °odic force; °Reich.

ouija board. Derived from the French *oui* (yes) and the German *ja* (yes). A board on which the letters of the alphabet are printed and used in conjunction with a planchette or pointer mounted on ball bearings. The fingers of one or more persons rest lightly on the planchette and a °spirit is invoked and asked questions. The °spirit is supposed to foretell events or give warnings. At either end of the board are the words 'yes' and 'no', and when questions are asked, the pointer runs over the surface and spells out the words. Not everyone can activate a planchette, but those with strong mediumistic powers can make it move with great speed and force.

Ousby, W.J. (1904–). Born in Liverpool, England. He wrote psychological articles while working as Advertising Manager of *World's Press News*. He left Fleet Street to become an industrial psychological

48. W. J. Ousby

consultant and specialized in psychoanalysis. He lectured and ran classes on self-hypnosis in London, Australia and New Zealand. He spent 8 years in Africa, mostly on safari, where he investigated °witch doctors and °ju-ju. He then trained in °yoga in India, investigated °fire walking and various methods of °trance and, as a result, he is an acknowledged authority on °hypnosis and self-hypnosis. He practises in Harley Street, London, and is the author of *Self-Hypnosis and Scientific Self-Suggestion* and *The Theory and Practice of Hypnotism*; °ill. 48.

Ouspensky, P. D. (1878–1947). °Gurdjieff's best-known pupil and a philosopher in his own right, whose books *Tertium Organum* and *A New Model of The Universe* gained him a place in the front rank of thinkers. His interest in the °occult led him to seek out °Gurdjieff, with whom he worked for 8 years. The difference between the two men is that Ouspensky is lucid when expounding his philosophy of Man in relation to the Universe, whereas °Gurdjieff is often cryptic and obscure. The two men were opposites but complementary. Their association was discontinued when Ouspensky quarrelled with °Gurdjieff and continued to delve more deeply into the °occult, which he dealt with in his last book *In Search of The Miraculous*, published after his death, in 1948.

P

Palladino, Eusapia (1854–1918). Born in Naples, Italy, she was one of the most remarkable °mediums of modern times. She was investigated by scientists in Italy, France, Germany and Britain: in 1892 by Prof. Schiaparelli, Brofferio, Gerso, °Richet, Lombroso and Aksakoff in Milan, in 1908 and 1909 by °Lodge, Dr Ochoroweiz and °Sidgwick in Cambridge, and by Prof. Morselli, Camille Flammarion and the Curies in Paris. The phenomena she demonstrated consisted of °materialization, °levitation, overturning heavy articles of furniture, and causing fluctuation by as much as 17lb in the °medium's weight. On one occasion, in broad daylight, the power from her body raised a table with a heavy Cararra marble top and propelled it towards Major A. H. Davis, an American millionaire, forcing him against the wall. Sir Fletcher Moulton and 4 servants tried to prevent the table from crushing him, without success, and only when the °medium's fingers touched it did the table return to its place in the middle of the room.

palmistry. An overall study of the hand: lines, shape, texture of the skin, feel, colour and the various markings, such as whorls, circles, squares, crosses, triangles, stars and dots. In the distant past palmistry was regarded as a serious study among the Chinese, Hindus, Jews and Egyptians, but it eventually fell into disrepute in the Middle Ages and was kept alive in Europe mainly by °gipsies, who learnt the art in India. °Desbarrolles was the first serious European palmist and placed palmistry on a semi-scientific footing. The oldest English works on palmistry are the manuscript of *Digby Roll IV* (*c.*1440), unearthed by Dr Derek J. Price of Christ's College, Cambridge, and a treatise by John Matham (*c.*1448–1449). Within recent years some eminent astrologers have read the palm with great accuracy: Henri Mangin in France, °Benham and Joseph Ranald in America, and Mme Mamlok of Berlin, who emigrated to America. °Cheiro also helped to place palmistry on a more scientific footing when he told London's Scotland Yard that the imprint of a palm they had was that of a mur-

palmistry

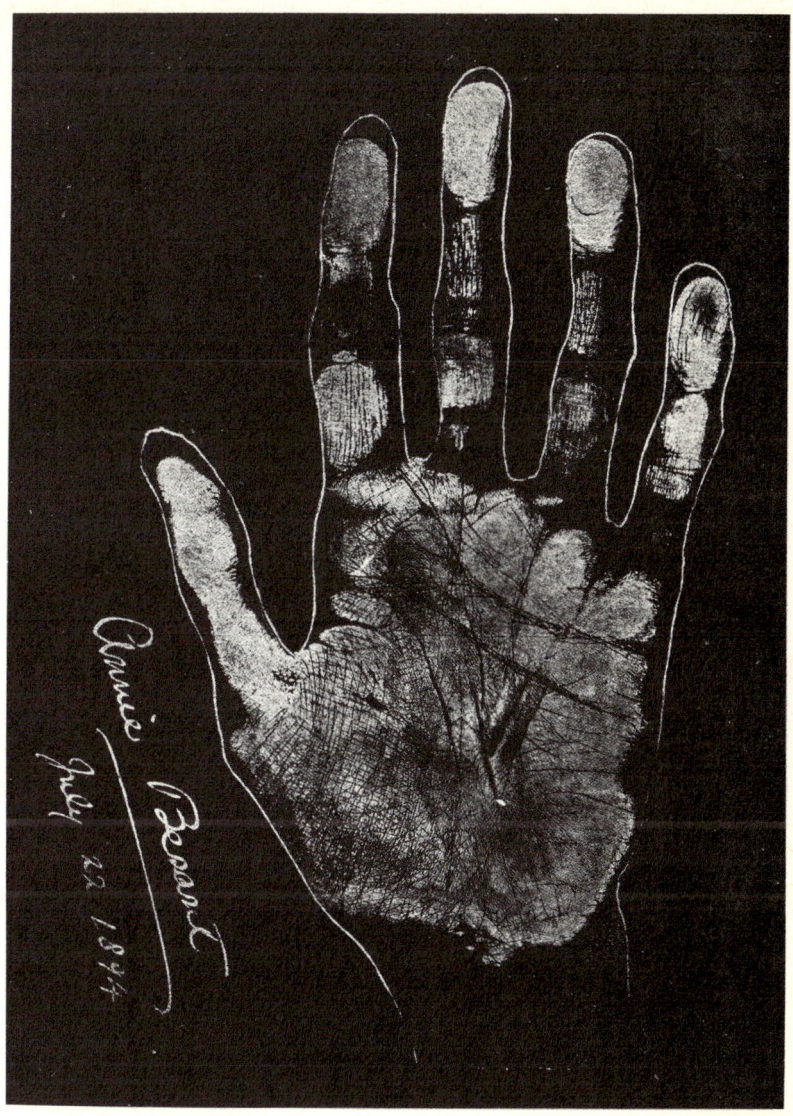

49. The hand of Annie °Besant, showing the lines that are read in palmistry.

derer. °Jaquin carried on this tradition and even persuaded the police to collaborate with him. He was concerned mainly with the study of character, latent ability, and the tendency to crime and disease. Later Mir °Bashir arrived in Britain, set up as a consultant, collaborated with medical men and was able to demonstrate that a disease which is latent in the body shows in the hand. In the East palmistry has always been respectable and, though there are thousands of charlatans, the leading practitioners are accorded the status enjoyed by medical specialists in Britain. °Gandhi and °Abayakoon combine °astrology with palmistry, as the arts are complementary, and °Abayakoon can determine the exact hour of birth by an examination of the hand. As with medicine, however, results depend largely on the skill with which the lines, marks, etc., are interpreted (diagnosed). We know as the result of thousands of experiments that the effects of the °subconscious are imprinted on the hand. A number of physicians in Britain are interested in the lines on the palm and their relation to health: Dr Julian Verbov of St Bartholomew's Hospital, C.S. Mellor at Manchester University, Drs David Lewis and Cyril Clarke at the Northern Hospital, Liverpool, Dr E.B. Ford at the Genetics Laboratory, Oxford University, Dr W. Stevenson of the Institute of Experimental Psychology, Oxford, Dr Charlotte Wolffe and others. °Jaquin said 30 years ago, 'During the past 4 or 5 years I have been able to detect some hundreds of cases of cancer in the early stages of development, and by sending people for treatment the ultimate development of an extensive cancer malignancy has been prevented.' India remains the hub of the world of palmistry. Twenty years ago *Sankhya*, the Indian journal of statistics, stated that a rough census in Calcutta revealed that 63 per cent of the population possesses °horoscopes and 60 per cent have had their hands read; °ill. 49.

pantheism. The doctrine that God and the universe are synonymous; God is everything and everything God; the heathen worship of all gods.

Paracelsus (1495–1541). Aureolus Philippus Theophrastus Bombastus von Hohenheim was born near Maria-Einsiedeln, Switzerland. At one time appointed town physician at Basle he was later lecturer in Medicine at Basle University in 1526, where he incurred the displeasure of the authorities by lecturing in German, instead of in the traditional Latin, and by his wholesale condemnation of renowned writers on medicine in the past, such as Galen and Avicenna. He wrote in language that was allegorical, mystical and symbolic; his vocabulary was complex and obscure, and as a result he was much misunderstood. Many achievements stand to his credit, however, for he was the first to diagnose and write on miner's disease, to establish the relationship between cretinism and goitre, to use mineral baths to cure, and to note the geographical differences in diseases. His views on °alchemy, in which he was adept, were expounded in a learned treatise. Paracelsus was a pioneer of modern psychology for he believed in the power of imagination, which could be disciplined to become a prime instrument in medicine; for without faith, which requires imagination, few cures are possible. He combined psychology, °phrenology, °physiognomy, °astrology and philosophy in his practice, which was outstandingly successful. In *De Rerum Natura* he discussed the influence of the imagination on the passions of the body, even on the unborn child. In *Doctrine of Signatures* he maintained that the planets influence men by their common magnetism, and that the °vibrations emanating from every object surrounding Man have either a beneficial or a harmful effect. He said he learnt more by mingling with the common people and from experience than from all the books in the University library. He was to medicine what Luther was to religion. His iconoclastic views earned him the title 'Firebrand of Medicine', and he is recognized as one of the most forceful figures of the Renaissance; °ill. 50.

50. Paracelsus. 19th-century engraving

parapsychology. A general term inclusive of supernormal phenomena, both physical and psychical; spiritualistic phenomena in general, including °telepathy, °clairvoyance, etc.

Parapsychology Foundation. Founded by °Garrett in 1951 as a non-profit-making educational organization dedicated to the support of impartial scientific inquiry into the nature and working of the human mind. The Foundation, based in England, publishes its own bi-monthly journal, *Parapsychology Review*, holds an annual conference on °psychic research and has a specialized library of some 7,500 volumes which is open to the public. It also publishes a series of monographs by researchers into the °psychic. °Garrett died in 1971 and the current President is Mrs Eileen Coly, her daughter.

Peden, Alex (?–1686). Born in Galloway, Scotland, he was a contemporary of the °Brahan Seer. In 1686 Patrick Walker covered 1,000 miles in Scotland and Ireland tracking down Peden's °prophecies from witnesses. Among other things Peden predicted the Irish Rebellion, the Siege of Londonderry, the Battle of the Boyne, the date of his own death and that of Charles II, and the fact that the King's body would be exhumed and reburied. Though not as well known as the °Brahan Seer, his °prophecies were every bit as startling and accurate.

pendulum. A small metal weight attached to a silken thread used in °psychometry to determine the sex of eggs, indicate the presence of minerals, water, oil, etc. The method is popular among chicken breeders in Japan and elsewhere. When hung over a map it will swing in the direction of minerals, water or oil and is a form of °dowsing. Some say it will even answer questions, such as, 'In which area shall I find a house?' and if placed over a map will indicate the direction and street. Though unscientific, the method has been proved correct so often that it should be given serious consideration; °radiesthesia.

Perryman, A.E. Known as Mme Faustina, she was a highly developed British clairvoyant, who functioned from early in the 20th century until the 1930s. Knowledge of her gift came when her mother, a daughter of Count Leon Phasavent, a Castilian, lay dying in Harrogate. She made many accurate °predictions; °clairvoyance.

Peters, Vout. A clairvoyant practising in London before the First World War who was remarkable for the accuracy of his °predictions. There was nothing vague about the things he saw. For instance, his predictions to Robert Hichens, the author, were photographic in description. Douglas Hunt was one investigator who checked, cross-checked and bore witness to Peters's extraordinary powers; °clairvoyance.

phantom. Illusion, unreality, °apparition, °ghost, spectre, °spirit.

Phasmatological Society. British group studying meteors, °phantoms, °apparitions and anything visionary.

philosopher's stone. A heavy, yellow, easily divisible substance, shining like powdered glass which, if projected upon much larger quantities of base metal, will convert them into silver or gold. Its origin goes back to Ancient Egypt, where Hermes was thought to have founded the science of °alchemy. In his *Book of the*

Revelations of Hermes °Paracelsus, the 16th-century physician, says that the stone contains the spirit of truth and cannot be understood without the instruction of the Holy Ghost: 'It heals all dead and living bodies without medicine ... and converts all inanimate bodies into gold.' A solution of the stone in spirits or wine is supposed to purge the body, cleanse it of all impurities and restore youth.

Phrenological Society, British. It was founded in 1886 by Lorenzo N. Fowler, the publisher, who was its first President. The Society was closed in 1967, but there are still thousands in Britain who believe in °phrenology and medical students at University College, London, are lectured on the fundamentals by Dr Edwin Clarke.

phrenology. The scientific study or theory of the mental faculties originated by the Germans °Gall and °Spurzheim, who said that the mental powers of individuals consist of separate faculties, each having its origin and location in a definite area of the surface of the brain, and this determines the shape of the skull. By feeling the contours of the head with the fingers, the phrenologist can estimate with accuracy the nature of the individual, his talents, and the strengths and weaknesses of his character. Phrenology has been used with success to discover where the talents of children lie in order to guide them in the right direction.

physiognomy. The art of judging character and disposition from the features of the face or the form and lineaments of the body generally. The face and its expression change not only with age, but also with the way one thinks and acts, and emotions show themselves plainly in the features. The study includes that of the eyes, which are one of the most revealing parts.

pineal gland. Gland of unknown function behind the third ventrical of the brain; third °eye.

Piper, Leonora (1857–1950). Born in Boston, Massachusetts, USA, her gift as a °medium was discovered at the age of 8 when she felt a sharp blow on the ear, followed by a hissing noise, and a voice saying, 'Aunt Sara not dead, but with you still'. A few days later came the news that her aunt had passed over at that very instant. At 22 she married William Piper and soon after visited Dr J. R. Cocke, a blind professional °medium renowned for his diagnostic ability and cures. On her second visit, she realized that she too was °psychic. Her revelations while in °trance were so numerous that they would fill volumes and so accurate that they convinced °James of Harvard, °Hodgson, °Myers and other sceptics. In the words of °James she was 'the one white crow that proves not all crows are black'.

pixie. A supposed supernatural being akin to a °fairy.

poltergeist. Derived from the German *polter* (noise) and *geist* (ghost). A °spirit that makes its presence felt by noises and sometimes by violent action. There are a number of theories about poltergeists: 1. that the human °psyche operates outside the body, causing this phenomenon; 2. that they are examples of °psychokinesis; 3. that they are usually associated with unhappy or mentally disturbed adolescents; 4. that they are persons no longer living, who for some reason cannot rest; 5. that all such manifestations are fraudulent. °Occult literature contains thousands of authenticated cases of poltergeists and their activities.

Pond, Philip. Current editor of *Prediction*, the leading °occult magazine in Britain.

prediction. The foretelling of events, trends, illnesses, etc., derived from the Latin *prae* (before) and *dicere* (to say or foretell). Prediction is the result of logical reasoning and deduction from facts, and is used by astrologers, palmists, phrenologists, etc., and is not the outcome of °inspiration, °intuition or °clairvoyance; °astrology; °palmistry; °phrenology.

premonition. A warning of subsequent events, not based on factual evidence or logical deduction; °sixth sense.

Price, Harry (1881–1948). Son of a wealthy British paper manufacturer in whose office he worked as a youth and whose mills he inherited, thus enabling him to give almost his entire attention to psychical research. His biography, *Search For Truth* by Dr Paul Tabori (1942), provides information on his activities. He devoted himself to a search for the truth and the exposure of fake °mediums and clairvoyants. Though known to the general public mainly for his investigation of ghostly phenomena in °Borley Rectory, his experiments with °Schneider and his collaboration with R.S. Lambert in the case of °Geoff the Talking Mongoose were only incidents in a busy life. He was editor of the magazine of the University of London Council for Psychical Investigation, Chairman of the National Film Library, council member of the Shakespearean Film Society and other bodies. He founded and equipped the first laboratory in Britain for the scientific examination of abnormal phenomena and formed the Harry Price Library of Magical Literature (20,000 volumes) in the University of London. He wrote numerous books, pamphlets and articles on the subject and did more than many to interest the public in °psychic phenomena and place them on a scientific footing. He probed every aspect of °extra-sensory perception, °apports, °fire walking, °materialization, °mediums, °poltergeists, °ghosts, etc.; °ill. 51.

51. Harry Price in the National Laboratory of Psychical Research, London, 1927

prophecy. Derived from the Latin *propheta* (one who speaks and interprets the will of God). Prophecies are not based on facts or reasoning but on inspired revelations. They are made by people with °second sight or by °mediums in a state of °trance. Though often accurate, they have no scientific basis and one cannot be instructed in the art. Colloquially the words prophecy and °prediction are interchangeable.

psi. °Extra-sensory perception (ESP). Psi is the twenty-third letter of the Greek alphabet and is now used to describe °psychic phenomena in general, that is, experiences for which there are no logical explanations and to which no physical cause can be attributed. It covers the entire field: °clairvoyance, °dowsing, °dream predictions, °ghosts, °premonitions, °prophecies, °second sight, °thought reading and all forms of extra-sensory communication; °Rhine.

psyche. Originally meant the principle of life, but is used generally as equivalent to mentality or as a substitute for the mind or soul, as distinct from the body.

psychic. From the Greek word for soul or life; one who is susceptible to spiritual influence.

psychic healing. The power to heal by the laying-on of hands through the projection of °vibrations, often at a distance, which many healers possess. No one knows exactly how °psychic healing takes place. °Edwards, °Turner, Finbarr Nolan and William Macmillan (1904–1959)

psychic surgery

believe they possess some power which flows through their hands into the bodies of the sick, though none can explain how this happens. Faith in a deity plays no part in the healing process, for they have cured agnostics and atheists. Others, such as Dr Christopher Woodard, Dr Rebecca Beard and the famous surgeon, Dr °Carrel, believe that faith is necessary. Pastor Jeffreys invariably started healing sessions with prayers and hymns to set the healing °vibrations in motion. Psychic healers come from all walks of life and no medical qualifications are needed; in fact, until comparatively recently both the medical profession and the churches (with the exception of the Roman Catholics) opposed psychic healing. Most healers discover their gift by accident, as did Lady Clerk, wife of Sir George Clerk, British Ambassador in Paris, who cured more than 500 people and was sent incurable cases by French doctors, and as did Mary Rogers, wife of ex-MP George Rogers, who cured of severe arthritis among others, John Lyle, Chairman of Tate & Lyle. The art of psychic healing is as old as civilized man. Five centuries before Christ, Asclepius performed similar °miracles. He founded a cult in Athens and °mysticism flourished. There were numerous healing cults, outside the orthodox school of Hippocrates, which had their temples and who wrought so-called miracles: Mithras, Serapis, Cybele, Osiris, Dionysus and others; °psychic surgery.

psychic surgery. Surgical operations performed without the use of instruments. Psychic surgeons, such as °Chapman, cure by distant healing, the laying-on of hands and psychic surgery. One of the best-known psychic surgeons was Arigo, a Brazilian who was killed in a car accident in 1972 at the age of 49. On some days he cured as many as 300 patients, diagnosing and treating them within minutes. Occasionally he performed minor operations with a pocket knife. *Time* magazine stated that 'he treated almost every known ailment and most of his patients not only survived but actually improved or recovered'. Arigo received impressive commendations from leaders in the field of °parapsychology and many of his cures were confirmed by Dr Henry Puharich, formerly of the New York Medical Centre, who testified to his powers at a conference on parapsychological medicine held at Stanford University, USA, attended by 400 doctors, engineers and biophysicists. In the Philippines a number of psychic surgeons operate regularly at the Bayview Hotel, Manila, where patients from every corner of the world are treated. Employing hands only, they open up the abdomen and other parts, remove tumours and diseased organs and cut out cancer of the breast. Faith is needed, but operations are said to be painless and leave no scars. As there are more than 500 spiritual healers in the Philippines inevitably some are fraudulent, but it seems that sleight-of-hand is unlikely. Donna Dora, also a Brazilian, has cured almost every disease in the medical encyclopedia, sometimes healing as many as 600 a day by laying-on of hands. Twice each week she does psychic surgery, for which she refuses to accept money or gifts, even from the wealthy. Her operations have been photographed by *Noticias Populares* and have been reported and commented on in *Die Andere Welt*. She uses no instruments but, unlike other psychic surgeons, wounds made by her fingers do not heal at once.

psychokinesis. The movement of objects by mental power; °poltergeist; °telekinesis.

psychometry. The faculty of divining from physical contact or proximity only the quality or properties of an object, or of persons or things that have been in contact with an object. Psychometry is based on the theory that all things, living and inanimate, radiate °vibrations which sensitives such as °mediums are able, by a process as yet undetermined, to translate into future events. The word was coined in 1842 by J.R. Buchanan, lecturer at an American medical college, when he found that drugs and metals had a psychological effect on himself. In practice, a °medium is handed an object, such as a wrist watch or ornament worn near the body, and by impinging his mind on this he (or she) is able to tune in to °vibrations emitted by the sitter, which relay information quite unknown. Often a psychometrist will give the history of the object and some aver that this is a form of °telepathy. Lost articles, valuable documents, gems, etc., have been traced by psychometry; °dowsing; °pendulum; °radiesthesia.

psychotherapy. The treatment of disorders by psychological methods. According to E. Fuller Torrey in *The Mind Game*: *Witch-Doctors and Psychotherapists*: 'My experiences working with °witch-doctors taught me that I was using the same mechanisms for curing my patients as they were – and not surprisingly, I was getting the same results.' There is nothing in psychotherapy that was not known thousands of years ago to °witch doctors in S. America, Red Indian °medicine men, °yogis and the practitioners of *ayurvedic* medicine in India, and the priests in Ancient Egypt and Greece. The idea that psychotherapy is comparatively new and was the discovery of °Freud, Adler and °Jung is no longer accepted.

Pyramid, Great. At Giza, one of the 70 or more pyramids built by the Egyptian Pharaohs, it may be

pyramid prophecy

entered through a triangular opening high up on one of its sides. At certain times of the year the rays of some stars penetrate through this opening and, if mirrors are fixed in the path of these rays, they will reflect into the corridor on to apparatus which enables observations to be taken. The passages, ascending and descending, were precisely cut to mathematical formulae and their measurements are said to reveal the future of the human race for the next 2,000 years. Certain of the measurements show the exact distance from the earth to the sun, the earth's polar diameter, and the value of Pi; °pyramid prophecy.

pyramid prophecy. The 3 major pyramids in Egypt were built during the reign of Cheops, Chephren and Mycerinus. Research into the Great °Pyramid of Giza started in 1859 when John Taylor, a mathematician and publisher, established the fact that the unit of measurement used was the polar diameter inch, which is substantially the same as the British and American inch, and he declared that the Great °Pyramid was built for the purpose of carrying a divine revelation. Belief in this hidden knowledge and prophecy goes back to the 10th century when Masoudi, an Arab writer, said that 'Surid, one of the Kings of Egypt before the Flood, built the 2 great pyramids . . . He ordered the priests to deposit within them accounts of their wisdom and requirements in the different arts and sciences . . . The King deposited the positions of the stars and their cycles, details of every future event which would take place in Egypt . . . the plans of the stars and historical and prophetic records.' The calculations of Profs Breasted and Piazzi Smith, Astronomer Royal of Scotland, give clues to its prophetic content and Dr Davidson shows in his book, *The Great Pyramid: Its Divine Message*, how these measurements can be applied. He was convinced that the Great °Pyramid was not merely a tomb but an instrument of °prophecy, and the various passages were keys to the future. His theory has been confirmed from independent sources, such as Marsham Adams in his study of the °*Book Of The Dead*. According to him, the passage-system of the Great °Pyramid is an astronomical time clock of 6,000 years of history in periods of 1,000 solar years and altogether the Pyramid contains prophecies which cover a period of 50,000 years. Some of the conclusions arrived at by the pyramidologists – the British are the lineal descendants of the Ten Tribes; the Danes are descended from the sons of Dan; the Irish were originally Israelites; Edward VIII was the hundredth descendant of David – are open to doubt, but even so the Great °Pyramid is an invaluable repository of prophecy and truth.

R

radiesthesia. The art of detecting and diagnosing disease by passing the hands over the body, based on the theory that disease comes from a disturbance of the balance of energy radiating from the organic cells and that the wave-lengths of radiations emitted by the body change during varying states of health. Some practitioners use the °pendulum instead of hands and a few, such as Abbé Mermet and Dr Moineau, claim to be able to cure disease under certain conditions. Dr Moineau has used the °pendulum to diagnose pregnancy during the first week and Abbé Mermet says that he can detect the precise organ that is diseased. Radiesthesia may be called scientific °clairvoyance; °Besson.

radionics. Often confused with °radiesthesia, it is based on the same theory; it does not depend, however, on °clairvoyance. Radionics is a science which deals instrumentally with radiations of all forms of matter but more especially with human radiations. Applying it in diagnosis and treatment of disease can be carried out by physical irradiation or distant radiation. It should be clearly understood that radionic diagnosis is not a diagnosis of the physical body and should not be interpreted in the physical sense. The apparatus has been developed to use the thought of the skilled operator as a probe in determining the basic causes of ill-health even if they be psychological in origin. The same principle applies in the diagnosis and treatment of plants and crops, whether on a large or small scale. An electrical instrument containing a number of magnetic coils is used, which tunes in to the emitted °vibrations, enabling the disease to be detected and diagnosed. Then °vibrations are sent out by the machine to alleviate or cure often over considerable distances. The first to put forward the theory of °vibrations was Goethe, followed by °Reichenbach, who called the life radiation OD (°odic force). The American pioneer was Dr Abrams, whose work was carried on by Dr °Drown. Dr W. E. Boyd in Glasgow and Dr Guyon Richards in London were the medical pioneers in Britain, but no one did more work in this field than George de la Warr, who first studied homeopathy and then turned to acoustic therapy and °radiesthesia. Today radionics is accepted by the medical profession and many physicians collaborate with the practitioners at the de la Warr Laboratories and elsewhere.

Raphael (1795–1832). Early 19th-century astrologer, whose real name was Robert Cross Smith, he gave his name to *Raphael's Astronomical Ephemeris*, now used for astrological calculations; °astrology.

rebirth. °Reincarnation.

Reich, Dr Wilhelm (1897–1957). Brilliant American scientist and psychoanalyst who discovered a new kind of energy akin to static electricity with healing powers, which he labelled °orgone. An early collaborator with °Freud. °Orgone is bluish in colour, emanates from the sun and affects all living organs. Clouds and bodies of water accumulate in it and it is the best guarantee of health. Reich made blankets consisting of layers of inorganic and organic material to trap °orgone, which prevented and cured colds, rheumatism, arthritis and even polio. More than 80 per cent of his patients were cured, but he was hounded by the American Medical Association, prosecuted under the Pure Food and Drugs Act and, when he refused to curb his activities, he was jailed. He committed suicide in prison. He wrote 30 books including *Orgone Accumulator*, *The Cancer Biopathy*, *The Murder of Christ*, *The Function of The Orgasm*, and *Character Analysis*.

Reichenbach, Baron Karl von (1788–1869). Discoverer of °odic force.

reincarnation. Rebirth; it has never been scientifically verified, but circumstantial evidence in its favour is strong and it is part of the theory of °karma, which says that only as a result of development can there be complete union with the infinite. In each life one should overcome and reject defects in character and so evolve to a higher plane; or if one fails to do so, fall to a lower one. Reaching the final stage may take thousands of years and each must work his own salvation. In reincarnation the person either changes sex or acquires the characteristics of the opposite sex. The Greeks, who learned from the Hindu philosophers, gave evidence of their belief in reincarnation; so does Christianity obliquely, for there are innumerable passages that point to it in the Bible, e.g. the Resurrection; Christ was twice identified as Elijah (Elias); °transmigration.

Rele, Dr Vansant G., FCPS, LM & S. He was the author of *The Vedic Gods*, *The Mysterious Kundalini*, etc., and was the first Indian medical practitioner to make a specialized study of °yoga, theoretical and practical, during the Edwardian era.

His *Mysterious Kundalini* (in English) is a standard work on the subject.

Rensburg, Nicholas van (1862–1925). Born in Transvaal, he was the son of a farmer. As a child he gave proof that he could see into the future and later became an elder of the Dutch Reformed Church. In 1899, when the Boer War broke out and his people were rejoicing over their victories, he warned them that hundreds of farms would be burnt and men and women taken prisoner. In his diary General Hertzog wrote, 'He foretold a successful battle near Wolmaranstad and described how the enemy would move', which was accurate to the last detail. Rensburg prophesied that General de la Rey would extricate himself from a precarious position and win a great victory, which he did when he captured Field Marshal Lord Methuen and his entire staff. He prophesied de la Rey's death and told General Smuts that he would win the General Election in 1924. He was so accurate that the S. African Government came to rely on him but did not exploit his powers.

Rhine, Prof. J.B. (1895–). Greatest living authority on °ESP. Professor of Psychology, Duke University, South Carolina, USA, who caused a sensation in 1934 with his book *Extra-Sensory Perception*, now known as °psi or ESP. Duke University was the first university to establish a department of °parapsychology with Rhine as its head. He and his wife, Dr Louisa Rhine, carried out thousands of tests with °zener cards, in which percipients were asked to guess which of the cards the agent had chosen. Mass experiments were carried out with the help of students and one student actually recited the names of 25 cards in the pack correctly. Tests were also carried out with percipients in different buildings, the odds against correct results being about 1020:1. Tests were so successful that critics maintained that fraud must exist, so the tests were made foolproof. Even then uncannily correct guesses were made, so sceptics denounced Rhine and said his mathematics must be faulty. He then called in the American Institute of Mathematical Statistics, which confirmed his figures. He made many scientists consider °ESP seriously and he was followed by other investigators: °Thouless at Cambridge, °Soal in London and °Tyrrell. In 1938 Rhine published *New Frontiers Of The Mind*, followed by other books and a spate of articles on ESP.

Richet, Prof. Charles (1850–1935). Professor of Physiology at the Faculty of Medicine, Paris, where he met °Gurney and °Myers, who had gone there to study °hypnosis. He was President of the °Society for Psychical Research in 1905 when he said that °psychic phenomena should be accepted 'on the grounds for the evidence of their occurrence, not because they are in any way understood'. He was one of the investigators who was convinced that most of °Palladino's manifestations were genuine. He won the Nobel Prize for Physiology and Medicine in 1913.

Roberts, Estelle (1890–1970). Known now as 'the human telephone from the spiritual world', she was punished and called 'a little liar' when she said she saw a °spirit at the age of 10. °Swaffer said she was the most remarkable woman he had ever known. She was certainly a most versatile °medium, being fluent in °clairvoyance, °clairaudience, °healing by touch, °materialization, °psychometry, °trance oratory, °xenoglossia, °automatic writing and the production of °apports. People had faith in her because she was so accurate and she collaborated on many occasions with the police. In 1937, when a child named Mona Tynsley disappeared, she told them where the body would be found and pointed to the exact spot in the river where it lay submerged in a sack. She created history by giving a demonstration of °spiritualism in the British House of Commons. Her story is told in *Estelle Roberts: Forty Years A Medium.*

Rosicrucians. The Ancient Mystical Order Rosae Crucis (AMORC) has its origin in one of the mystery schools of secret wisdom in Ancient Egypt during the 18th dynasty (reign of Pharaoh Akhnaton, *c.* 1350 BC). Its first member-students met in the secret chambers of the Great °Pyramid, where they were initiated into the mysteries. Legend says that its adepts, masters and teachers imparted their wisdom to the builders of Solomon's temple. The first European book on the order appeared in Casse, Germany, in 1614 and in 1652 the book was introduced into England by Thomas Vaughan under the title *Fame and Confessions of Rosie-Crosse*, though some attribute the work to John Valentine Andrae. A few of their members emigrated to America in 1694 where they sought 'freedom of speech and the right to search for truth wherever it may be found'. They founded a colony at Ephrata, Pennsylvania, USA, where they built the first astronomical observatory in America and then the first paper mill. They also organized the first symphony orchestra and developed the first botanical garden. Some of the leading citizens, among them °Franklin and Jefferson, were members, and in Europe Michael Meier, Albertus Magnus, Roger Bacon, Jacob Boehme, John Heydon, Francis Bacon, Richard Fludd and °Ashmole were members of the order. The AMORC is independent and free from religious sectarianism. Members follow the dictates of their

runes

52. The Franks' Casket shows the figures surrounded by runic inscriptions (AD 700) (*British Museum. Crown Copyright*)

conscience, fight °superstition, ignorance and fear, and refrain from political controversy. The order is not a secret one and lodges and fraternal temples exist in many parts of the world. There are several rival groups of Rosicrucians: the Fraternity at San José was introduced into America by Dr R.S. Clymer; the AMORC began its activities under the philosopher Dr H. Spencer Lewis; the Rosicrucian Fellowship came into being under the German nobleman and °mystic Max Heindel, an astrologer of considerable ability, in 1909; the Society of Rosicrucians in New York was founded in 1909. All 4 claim to expound the true teachings publicly for the first time in America; each is refuted by the others and, though the AMORC has challenged its rivals to public debate, they have all refused. The Societas Rosicruciana in Anglia was given its present definite form by Robert Wentworth Little of England in 1886 and was founded on the ruins of the old German Association which he discovered during his researches.

runes. A set of stones engraved with °mystic symbols used by °mediums and other sensitives for seeing into the future. Each set consists of 8 stones of natural shape and colour cut with a given rune. The first, of yellowish hue and round, must be searched for, found, and engraved with a circle of 7 arrows; the second, greenish and inscribed with a curling wave design; the third, white, transparent, shaped like a bean and cut with 4 small crossed squares; the fourth, square, black and cut with a double cross; the fifth, purplish, rough, triangular in shape and inscribed with an ear of corn; the sixth, red and squarish, inscribed with crossed pointed arrows; the seventh, pale blue, ovoid and cut with interlocking circles; the eighth, triangular and cut with 3 birds in flight. Each stone relates to certain events and the reader can determine events from the pattern and place in which they fall; °ill. 52.

S

sacrifice. Primarily the slaughter of an animal or person as an offering to a deity.

salamander. Sprite of fire which appears as a globe over the sea or on the masts and rigging of vessels, known as St Elmo's fire. In the past salamanders were thought to be °spirits of the dead, but we now know that the phenomenon is caused by static electricity.

sand reading. A method of predicting practised mainly in Egypt and the Arab world. Sand is strewn on the ground and the diviner makes little holes in it, causing patterns from which the future is read. There are no books on it, for it is an abstruse art handed down from father to son. °Predictions are often astonishingly accurate.

Satyanarayana Sai Baba (1926–   ). Generally known as Sai Baba, he was born in Puttapuri, Mysore, South India, where he lives and works at the Prasanti Nilyam ashram (retreat). The son of Brahmins, he claims to be the °reincarnation of a Muslim saint, Sai Baba of Shiridi. He does not accept money or gifts for the help he gives, though how his ashram is financed is a mystery. He has the ability to produce food, money, jewels and other articles from the air. Once, when being entertained by a Mr Ramachandran who expected 50 guests, more than 1,000 turned up on hearing that Sai Baba was present. There was food for about 60 but he multiplied it till all had ample. In 1942 O. Partasaraty, a Madras businessman, and his family witnessed Baba's levitation up a hill and into a tall tree – a feat others claim to have witnessed at various times. Sai Baba also cured Partasaraty of asthma by giving him an apple to eat which he had materialized. He frequently materializes objects from the air and can transmute base metals into gold and rocks into sweetmeats. Each morning and afternoon he advises and helps those who seek his aid and his cures have ranged from cancer to the casting out of devils. He has also resuscitated the dead. A number of books have been written about him and his work, the best known being *Sanathana Sarathi* by Prof. N. Kasturi, former Principal of Mysore University, and *Sai Baba, Man of Miracles* by Howard Murphet. The prefix to his name, Satya, means truth, Brahman or the absolute; °alchemy; °apports; °materialization.

Savage, Jane (1879–). A °psychic born in New York State, USA, where she was a successful singer and teacher. On 22 September 1918 a man wearing the garb of an oriental priest suddenly appeared in front of her and made a number of °prophecies which she jotted down: 1. that the First World War would end before 15 November (the Armistice was signed on the 11th); 2. her husband would be decorated twice and return from Italy by Christmas; 3. the Kaiser would flee to a small country and die there; 4. that within 20 years an Austrian would get so much power that he would lead Germany into a second war which she would lose; 5. the USA would finance numerous countries; 6. the east and west coasts of America would be changed by earthquakes and tidal waves; 7. volcanoes under the Panama Canal would blow up and automatically open a Nicaraguan Canal; 8. Europe would rise like the phoenix; 9. labour and capital would clash and all classes would clamour for more money. She was also told of the economic crisis in 1929, the abdication of Edward VIII, and Japan's attack on America. All these °prophecies were printed in American newspapers.

Schneider, Willi (1903–) and Rudi (1908–1957). Famous °telekinetic °mediums between the wars, who gave sittings under the auspices of the °Society for Psychical Research and produced striking phenomena. Rudi produced, at a

53. Rudi Schneider aged twenty-one

scrying

distance, an invisible substance which had the power of absorbing infra-red rays, which did not appear on the negatives of films in which simultaneous flashlight photographs were taken. The experimental data obtained during sittings under stringent test conditions convinced observers of paranormal activity; °ill. 53.

scrying. °Crystal gazing.

seance. A sitting for the purpose of obtaining spiritistic or metaphysical phenomena; it is usually, though not always, a group with a °medium in a darkened room.

second sight. A supposed power by which occurrences in the future or things at a distance are perceived as if they were actually present. There is overwhelming evidence that some possess this power and can see what is hidden from normal mortals; °seer.

seer. One who sees into the future or makes prophetic utterances for which there are no logical grounds; °clairvoyance; °prophecy; °second sight.

sensitives. Those affected by external influences not apparent to normal people; °clairvoyants; °mediums; °seers; °trance healers; °macumba; °Serato.

Sepharial (Dr Walter Gorn–Old) (1864–1929). One of the most successful astrologers to practise during the Edwardian era in England, who also read the cards, gazed into the °crystal and was adept at °numerology. His most remarkable °predictions, published 15 years before the events in his book *A Manual of Astrology* (1903), stated that: 1. the German empire would vanish; 2. the Kaiser would never be a popular monarch and would lose almost all his possessions; 3. that he would be forever quarrelling; 4. that his wife would die; 5. that it was not impossible that his territory would fall into the hands of France and Russia; 6. that he would die suddenly of a heart affliction. He wrote numerous other books on °astrology.

Serato. An area of the Brazilian hinterland known as the country of °seers who practise °macumba.

Serios, Ted. A poorly educated, unemployed bell-hop born in Kansas City, USA whose remarkable powers were discovered in his forties. He is able to project photographic images on to Polaroid film by staring into the lens of a camera with intense concentration. The pictures reproduced on film – the gardens of the Taj Mahal, the Pentagon, dome of the White House, portico of the Natural History Museum, Chicago, and others – were placed in opaque envelopes on which he concentrated before gazing into the lens of a camera. Some of the first tests were made under the supervision of Curtis Fuller, editor of *Fate* magazine and President of the Illinois Society for Psychic Research (ISPR).

Then Pauline Oehler, Vice-President of the ISPR, persuaded Dr Julius Eisenbud, a psychiatrist and psychoanalyst, to investigate, which he did. Though none of the °thought photographs are exact reproductions of those that Serios concentrated upon in the envelopes, all possess salient features of the originals: crenellated roofs, doric columns, domes, etc., and have striking similarities. Scores of experiments are described, with illustrations, in *The World of Ted Serios* by Julius Eisenbud. The pictures produced are among the most amazing examples of °psychokinesis.

serpent worship. There are tribes in Africa, Brazil and India who worship snakes. In Malaysia the belief exists that the hamadryad (king cobra) has the power to enter the vital organs of humans who harm it and can poison them without any visible signs of attack. If a hamadryad is killed by a man, its mate will seek the killer and take its revenge. It is believed in Brazil that Col Fawcett, the explorer, died because an enemy looked at him with 'a bad eye' and sent a snake to kill him. Snakes are worshipped, fed and cared for by such tribes. People in the Sunderbunds, in the Ganges delta, have no fear of the most poisonous reptiles; they treat them as friends and are immune to their poison.

shadow reading. In India and perhaps elsewhere there are men who can predict the future by reading a client's shadow at any time between 9 am and 4 pm. First the full shadow is measured, then accurate measurements are taken of the palm and fingers with a ruler, a *shamku* (a sort of geometrical compass) and a sundial. The °seer makes calculations and consults ancient scripts written on °palm leaves in Hindi, Ardhmadghi and Sanskrit, which have been passed down through countless generations. There are 2 types of leaves – written and carved – some more than 1,000 years old. There are no books on the subject that the beginner can consult, for the art is passed down from father to son. One of the leading exponents in India is Shantiprasad Sharma cf Patan, North Gujarat.

Shamanism. Primitive religion of the Ural-Altaic peoples of Siberia, in which all the good and evil in life is believed to be brought about by °spirits which can be influenced by the *shamans* or priests. Eskimos and American Indians in the north-west of America also believe in shamanism.

sibyl. A woman of Ancient Rome who was reputed to possess powers of °prophecy and °divination; °Delphic oracle; °oracle.

Sidgwick, Prof. Henry (1838–1900). Professor of Moral Philosophy at Cambridge, he devoted a considerable amount of time to the investigation of °extra-sensory perception and

signs, occult

became the first President of the °Society for Psychical Research. He presented the SPR with 170 books which formed the nucleus of its library. His best-known work is *The Methods of Ethics*; °ill. 54.

signs, occult. Since time immemorial certain signs have been endowed with magical or lucky qualities. The 5-pointed star, also known as °Solomon's star, is one of the most ancient signs and is believed to be a protection against °witches. Three arrows crossed by diagonal lines is a

 five-pointed star

 fascine

 oriental cross

 circle cut by semi-circles

55. Occult signs

54. Prof. Henry Sidgwick

sign of unity and strength, as illustrated by the fascine, a cylindrical faggot of brushwood bound firmly together, later to become the symbol of Fascism. The journey of Man's soul through life is represented by 4 horizontal lines with a vertical line cutting them, forming an Oriental Cross which symbolizes

signs of the zodiac

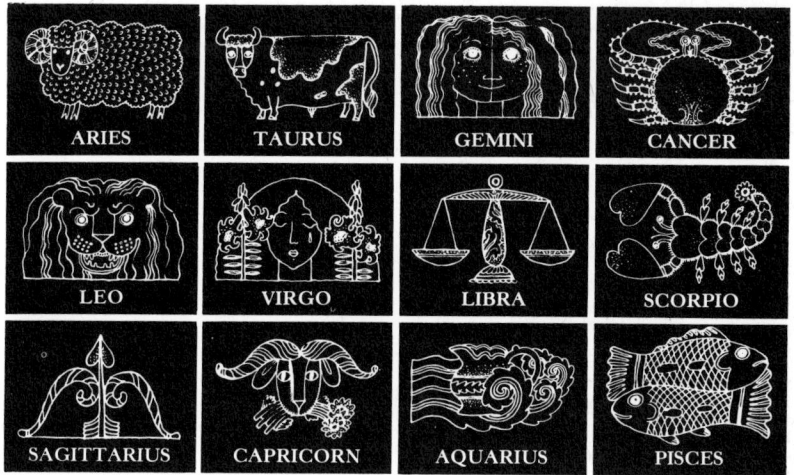

56. Signs of the zodiac

the soul's journey through earth, air, fire and water, till eventually it is purified and reaches light or self-realization. Another sign used to ward off evil °spirits is a circle cut at equal distances by semi-circles which are drawn in one movement to ensure that evil spirits cannot break through; °glyphs; °signs of the zodiac; °zodiac; °ill. 55.

signs of the zodiac. 1. Aries the Ram; 2. Taurus the Bull; 3. Gemini the Heavenly Twins; 4. Cancer the Crab; 5. Leo the Lion; 6. Virgo the Virgin; 7. Libra the Scales; 8. Scorpio the Scorpion; 9. Sagittarius the Archer; 10. Capricorn the Goat; 11. Aquarius the Water Bearer; 12. Pisces the Fishes; °astrology; °horoscope; °zodiac; °ill. 56.

sixth sense. A faculty of perception supposed not to depend upon any 'outward sense', instinct or intuition; a sense additional to and unconnected with the normal sense of sight, hearing, smell, taste and touch.

sleep-walking. °Somnambulism.

Smith, Joseph (1806–1844). Son of puritanical New England parents, he was born near Rochester, USA. Confused when his family was caught up in a religious revival, one day, after reading James 1:5, he retired to the woods to ask for divine guidance. Darkness fell and while he was engrossed in prayer a

Soal

personage appeared to him in a pillar of light. Later, on the evening of 21 September 1823, while praying, the personage again appeared enveloped in light, announced himself as the °angel Moroni and said that God had work for him to do. The °angel said that a message inscribed on the golden plates of Mormon, a prophet, had been delivered by the Saviour to the ancient inhabitants of America and now lay under a rounded stone on a hill 4 miles from Palmyra. Smith visited the spot and unearthed the 'book', but it was another 4 years before the message, written in Egyptian, Chaldaic, Assyrian and Arabic, was translated. It revealed the 'true' teachings of Christ, which now form the basis on which members of the Church of Jesus Christ of Latter-Day Saints (commonly called Mormons) run their lives. The Mormons were hounded and persecuted, and when Joseph Smith and his brother were assassinated, his mantle fell on °Young, who led the Mormons west to Utah, where they built Salt Lake City.

Soal, Dr S.B. He was famous for his successful card guessing experiments between 1927 and 1929 with the °medium Blanche Cooper, which were strangely negative, and further experiments between 1934 and 1939 with 160 people who altogether made 28,350 guesses on °zener cards. After initial failures, he analysed

57. Dr S. B. Soal

thousands of guesses and was amazed to find that two of his percipients achieved scores far greater than could be accounted for by guesswork; °Rhine; °ill. 57.

Society For Psychical Research (SPR). Founded by a group inquiring into psychical occurrences in the middle of the 19th century and was an offshoot of the °Ghost Society at Cambridge during 1851–1852. Among the original members were E.W. Benson, later Archbishop of Canterbury; J.B. Lightfoot and Foss Westcott, who became bishops; and Hort, who was Professor of Divinity. Later °Sidgwick and F. °Myers joined and with others formally founded the SPR. The Society was strengthened by °Gurney, Lord Rayleigh, Miss E.M. Balfour, Dr Arthur Myers, °Crookes, °Barrett, °Moses and A.R. Wallace. Sir Charles Oman, one of the leading lights of the °Phasmatological Society, gave considerable help. Early Council Members (1887) and Honorary Members were: Gladstone (Prime Minister), °Balfour (later Prime Minister), 8 Fellows of the Royal Society (A.R. Wallace, Couch Adams, Lord Rayleigh, °Lodge, A. Macalister, J. Venn, Balfour Stewart and J.J. Thomson); 2 bishops; Lord Tennyson, John Ruskin, Prof. Dodgson (Lewis Carroll), J.A. Symonds and William Bateson. The objects of the SPR are to: 1. examine the nature and extent of any influence which may be exerted by one mind on another, apart from any generally recognized mode of perception; 2. study °hypnotism and the forms of so-called mesmeric °trance, with its alleged insensibility to pain; °clairvoyance and other allied phenomena; 3. critically revise °Reichenbach's researches and inquire whether such organisms possess any power of perception beyond a highly exalted sensibility of the recognized sensory organs; 4. investigate reports based on strong testimony regarding °apparitions at the moment of death, or otherwise, or regarding disturbances in houses reputed to be haunted; 5. inquire into psychical phenomena called spiritualistic, with an attempt to discover their causes and general laws; 6. collect and collate existing material bearing on the history of these subjects. The aim of the Society is to approach these problems without prejudice or prepossessions of any kind, and make an objective inquiry. Though °Barrett is generally regarded as the founder of the SPR, the inspiration came from Edmund Dawson Rogers, a well-known journalist and spiritualist who, in a discussion with °Barrett at his home in Finchley, suggested the formation of a society 'to attract some of the best minds which had hitherto held aloof from the pursuit of the inquiry into °spiritualism and °psychic phenomena'. During a tour of America in 1884 °Barrett aroused interest in °psychic phenomena among American scientists, who the following year formed an °American SPR under the presidency of Simon Newcomb, but soon °James became its leading light and in 1887 °Hodgson went out to take over the management. The British and American societies have since collaborated fruitfully.

solistry. The ancient art of foot reading. In China the symbols for the marks differ from those used in Indian and Persian solistry and are not connected with the °signs of the °zodiac or the planets but with birds, serpents, trees, flowers, books and other objects; °cartopedy.

Solomon's seal. The symbolical interlaced triangles adopted by the °Theosophical Society as its seal; known in India as the sign of Vishnu, the second person in the Hindu trinity, the others being Brahma and Siva (or Shiva). Vishnu is identified with the sun: the all-pervader, the sustaining life of God and the symbol of knowledge; occult °signs °ill. 55a.

somnambulism. Walking or carrying out other activities while asleep; at one time applied to certain hypnotic phenomena under the name 'artificial somnambulism'. We now know that there is no connection, but the causes of somnambulism are still uncertain. During sleep-walking people have performed hazardous feats which they would not have attempted if awake, such as negotiating high, narrow ledges in safety, climbing trees (one woman did so in the nude), or cutting down a field of nettles. Sleep-walking is a mystery to the medical profession and to all who have studied the phenomenon.

sorcery. The use of °magic or enchantment; °witchcraft.

soul. The whole mind, which includes the powers of will, love and thought, and not merely the thinking mind. The soul persists from one °reincarnation to another and is independent of the habits and emotions of the lower mind. As used by theosophists, soul may be defined as °spirit manifesting itself objectively, that is, through substance of different grades. Cosmically it may be *buddhi* or the bliss-soul, or *mahat* or the intelligent soul, or the astral light, which is the lowest division of the universal soul. Microcosmically it may be *buddhi* or *manas* or °*kama*.

spell. An invocation by a °witch, wizard, °ju-ju man or some other adept at °magic which influences another, usually detrimentally. There are good spells as well as bad; the good protect against evil. °Amulets, °charms and other objects may have spells cast over them to influence and affect people.

spirit. *Atman*; the supreme underlying cosmic reality. Matter is the vehicle for the manifestation of the °soul on Earth and the °soul is the manifestation of the spirit.

spirit photography. William Mumler, an American engraver, took the first °spirit photographs in 1861. Since then thousands of experiments have been conducted and numerous spirit photographs taken, the most important being those of °Schneider and the Nad Kelly pictures taken in 1952. Michaela Kelly was sent into a deep °trance by Mr von Sealay, who then quickly cut a sheet of enlarging paper from a standard packet and placed it under her hands, which were flat on a table. When developed, a heavy figure wearing a shawl was seen, with the letters

NAD imprinted clearly on it. These referred to Nad or Naddie, the name by which her mother's housekeeper, who had died recently, was known.

spirit writing. Similar to °automatic writing except that spirit writing is done under the inspiration of some departed person, whereas in °automatic writing the control is not known, however both are inspirational. The spirit writer °Cummins used to sit at a table, make her mind blank and rest her hand on a block of foolscap; then her control, Astor, would announce the presence of a communicator and she would cover sheets of paper under his influence in the communicator's handwriting.

spiritualism. The belief that the °spirits of those who have passed over can communicate with the living, usually through a °medium, though also by other means; the system of doctrine or practices founded on this belief.

Spiritualist Association. In 1872 in London a small group under the leadership of W.T. Cooper, calling themselves the Spiritual Evidence Society, began investigating a new range of phenomena which promised insight into the nature of life and gave experimental data on man's °soul. By 1880 the group still only consisted of 30 members, for to belong invited social ostracism and sometimes business ruin. In 1890 Mr and Mrs Thomas Everitt joined the group, the latter being a °medium who could move objects without physical contact, produce °spirit writings, direct voice, and taps. The couple brought in many members, among them Leigh Hunt, who became Honorary Secretary, and Florence Marryat, the novelist, who bought an abandoned police court for their premises in 1891. In 1894 they moved to the Cavendish Rooms and in 1905 assumed the name Marylebone Spiritualist Association. Since then they have moved a number of times, growing larger and attracting thousands of members. Now the Association is an internationally recognized body with its headquarters in London, and is the most influential organization of its kind in the world.

Spurzheim, Dr Johann Gaspar (1776–1832). He made a close study of the brain and realized that the shape of the skull determined the type of brain beneath it. By running his fingers over a skull and measuring it with callipers, he was able to type people, point out their faults and indicate their talents. An amative person has a well-developed area of benevolence; in a rogue the organ of theft is larger than normal, etc. When he first lectured on °phrenology, he was ridiculed by his colleagues and denounced by the Church, but he made many disciples and, though doubters far outnumbered believers, there are many doctors and scientists who maintain that the principles enunciated by °Gall and Spurzheim have opened the door to a new and valuable study.

Stanhope, Lady Hester (1776–1859). Daughter of the Earl of Stanhope, who for a time kept house for her uncle, William Pitt in 10 Downing Street, till his death. She visited Brothers, a 'mad' °fortune-teller, in his cell in Bedlam and he prophesied that one day she would be crowned Queen of the East. When she was 30 she went abroad and travelled widely. In the desert an old man named Metta told her of the existence of a °magic book which predicted that a European woman would live at Mt Lebanon and have greater power than the Sultan. She obtained the book and read the °prophecy and ultimately, after many adventures, she rode between mutilated columns of marble into the ruined city of Palmyra where thousands of citizens flocked to hail her as Queen. She was self-educated, studied medicine, mathematics, °astrology, and dabbled in °magic, °necromancy, craniology and °physiognomy.

star of David. A 6-pointed star in an interlaced double triangle on the Shield of Judah. It is one of the most powerful °occult symbols as it signifies the eternal struggle between good and evil on the Earth. Positive and negative forces are combined in a single symbol to show that there is actually no distinction between positive and negative in the ultimate, both being part of the godhead. The star of David is sometimes confused with the °star of Solomon. It is now the national emblem of Israel and may be seen engraved on blocks of stone in the remains of the Capernaun synagogue where Jesus preached.

star of Solomon. A 5-pointed star which is geometrically symbolic of Man, the middle point being his head and the other four his arms and legs. This star is drawn in one movement, starting at the top and returning there; °ill. 58.

58. Star of Solomon

Steiner, Rudolf (1861–1925). Born in Kraljevec, on the Austro–Hungarian border, he was the originator of °anthroposophy, which is a way of life rather than a dogma. In his twenties he was invited to edit Goethe's scientific works for a special edition; in 1901 he became a spiritual teacher and for 10 years was a member of the °Theosophical Society, but broke away to form the

Anthroposophical Society (Wisdom of Man). He attached great importance to the spiritual life and built a theatre (Goetheanum) for the performance of mystery plays. He and his colleagues explored °etheric forces and proved the influence of Jupiter on tin, Saturn on lead, sun on gold, and moon on silver. He also proved by experiment the influence of the moon on growing plants. °Anthroposophy accepts °reincarnation but rejects °spiritualism because entry into spiritual life is made through enhanced °consciousness, not through submerged °consciousness. He was greatly influenced in his teens by a herb-gatherer who taught him the secret virtues of plants, their rightful place in the universal order of things and their relation to man. He broke from °theosophy because he was born a Catholic, was deeply impressed by ritual, and rejected the idea of a dogma of revelation imposed from without. Steiner founded schools in which the whole man is educated and where there is curative education for handicapped children. He defined °anthroposophy as a practical application of Christianity that should be known by its results. He inspired hundreds who work selflessly in a dozen different fields of service, and he also instituted eurhythmy, a form of dancing which expresses speech in movement. There are some 50,000 °anthroposophists scattered throughout the world.

stones. °Birthstones.

subconscious. A term employed, mainly by the French school of psychopathology, for processes of the same order as °conscious processes but occurring outside the personal awareness of the individual; often employed loosely, as equivalent to °unconscious. One of the 4 states of awareness. Few people realize the reasons for their actions and desires, and imagine that they control their own destinies. Many of the actions we perform, however, are due to underlying forces of which we have no cognizance and which are born in the subconscious mind. It is this *avidya* which must be dissipated, say theosophists and °yogis, first by concentration, then by °meditation and contemplation. Only in this way can we control our minds instead of letting our minds control us.

subliminal force. Below the threshold of perception; employed either of stimuli or of stimulus differences; also employed of the acquisition of a habit, where the learning itself is not °conscious.

Sufism. In Islam and in India in particular there is a bewildering diversity of orders, rituals and beliefs in which Hindu influence has played a considerable part, as it has in Sufism. Sufis are Muslim

°mystics whose aim is 'to lose themselves in God' by passing through 7 stations or levels of development by their own efforts, after which they receive 10 'states' from God which human endeavour cannot achieve. During °meditation they draw nearer to the infinite, and by love, hope, longing, intimacy, contemplation, a deep feeling of certainty and constant remembrance of God (*dhikr*) they become united with Him. When that happens there is a passing away of all human qualities and failings (*fana*). This is the same as °Buddha's doctrine of *nirvana* or the doctrine of liberation of the Ancient Hindus, except that in Sufism God is not regarded as a symbol but as the creator of life. The word sufi is derived from the Arabic *suf*, the woollen garment worn by the early followers of Sufism, which was condemned by ascetics who said it was worn in imitation of Jesus. Sufis prefer to dress in cotton as did the Prophet. In the 2nd century AD a group of ascetics in Kufa called *al-Sufiya* gathered for pious discussion and lived in convents, cells and grottoes in imitation of the Nestorians. Their services consisted of recitals of the Koran and other religious writings; at first they were ascetics but later turned, like the primitive Christians, to mystical love, which supplants fear as a motive. Sufis are fervent propagandists and the most advanced of all Muslim sects. The orthodox Muslims tried to suppress them but failed as their beliefs are firmly rooted in the Koran; they reject doctrinaire beliefs and follow the 'inner light'. In general they believe in a world of similitudes (*alam-al-mithal*), a world of images in which gross bodies from the material realm from below are transformed into subtle bodies or images. The human °spirit can rise to different levels and achieve freedom from the finite existence of this world.

sungma. A living °oracle of the Tibetan Church. Sungma means guardian or protector of religion. The bodies of sungmas are the abodes of malignant °spirits or the spirits of demonized heroes who, subdued by saintly lamas or high incarnations, have become the protectors of religion and manifest themselves involuntarily in their chosen abodes. Sungmas charge fees for prophesying, the amount depending on the importance of the °daemon and the wealth of the client, and it may be as much as 1,000 *tankas* (£50) or more. Questions are written on slips of paper and handed to the sungma who holds it above his head and answers with incredible rapidity, usually to the accompaniment of grunts and groans. The answers, usually vague and ambiguous, are interpreted by an attendant lama. Though there are many sungmas, genuine and fake; in Tibet, the 5 of real importance used to live in Lhasa and the head or State Oracle, Na Chung, was always consulted by the Dalai Lama. When performing, the sungma wears an elaborate robe decorated with gold brocade, the gift of some devout worshipper. While the priests chant, he buries his face in his hands to gain °intuition, then breathes some fragrant juniper smoke. A tall plumed iron hat weighing over 50lbs is placed beside him, then to the tune of trumpets and clashing cymbals the *chechin* (°daemon) enters his body. A lama places the heavy hat on his head, fastens it under his chin, and after a while the sungma starts to throw himself about and gyrate. A sword with a Mongolian steel blade is handed to him, which he twists into loops and knots as he sways, leaps and dances. Eventually, after a display of superhuman power, he sinks exhausted. Such is their frenzy that sometimes a sungma will disembowel himself. The steel swords twisted by them are highly prized and are hung above gates and doorways to ward off evil °spirits. Sungmas must lead abstemious lives; they must not eat chicken, pork or eggs, smoke or take snuff. There is no scientific reason to account for their superhuman strength and stamina during their displays in °trance.

sun worship. Strictly speaking there are no sun worshippers, though the Parsees, descendants of Persians who fled to India, regard the sun as a symbol of life and pay homage to it. The Aztecs, Incas and °Druids also regarded the sun as the symbol of life and they and other tribes scattered throughout the world erected megaliths, monoliths and sun temples. Sun worship was probably a Stone Age cult. Many megaliths show a definite orientation and were used for taking sun readings connected with a primitive form of °astrology, e.g. Stonehenge; °Zarathustra.

superconscious. The °yogi believes that Man has not a double, but a triple personality: the °conscious and the °subconscious being crowned by the superconscious – a term not yet recognized by psychologists. Superconsciousness is the fourth state of awareness, between wakefulness, sleep and dreams. In °yoga it is known as *turiya*, and superconscious knowledge is called *prajna* and is a higher form of knowledge than scientific truth because it is the result of perception; °unconscious.

superstition. A belief or system of beliefs based on imaginary connections between events, and incapable of being justified on rational grounds; a reserved belief in influences, agencies and forces whose existence is uncritically accepted; in the individual, the tendency to accept such beliefs and act upon them, e.g. that spilling salt, walking under ladders and opening an umbrella in the house is unlucky, that a horseshoe brings good luck and 7 is a lucky number.

Swaffer, Hannen (1879–1962). Born in Kent, he went to London as a reporter and worked for practically all his adult life for *The People*. He became convinced of the truth of °spiritualism. By his writings and exposure of fake °mediums, he did more than any man before to establish the truth and convince many people of some kind of existence in the hereafter. Originally Swaffer was a sceptic and it was only after he was given indisputable evidence, time and again, that he became a spiritualist.

swastika. The word is derived from the Sanskrit *svastika*, meaning well-being or good luck, and is a primitive symbol or ornament in the form of a cross with equal arms and limbs of the same length projecting at right angles from the ends of the arms, all in a clockwise direction. The arms of the Nazi swastika point in a counter-clockwise direction and it is generally accepted that this is an evil cross and an ill °omen. The swastika is carved prominently on temples in India where it originated, and in Ceylon, Burma and the Far East where the followers of Buddhism placed it; °signs; °ill. 59a, b.

Swedenborg, Emmanuel (1689–1772). Born in Stockholm, son of the Bishop of West Gothland, he was one of the most talented men of his time: physiologist, mechanic, mathematician, philosopher, inventor. Raised to the nobility in 1719, he changed his name from Swedborg to Swedenborg. His scientific work explains the system of nature in relation to the creation of animal life and is based on the process of energic emanation, similar to that propounded in the °Kabalah. It aroused clerical opposition but gained him many followers. After visiting London in 1743, he turned from material to spiritual science and began a series of direct communications of wisdom similar to those experienced by the Biblical prophets. So deeply impressed was he by these revelations that he resigned all his offices and devoted himself to intercourse with higher minds and refused all further appointments, though Charles XII continued to pay him his full salary as a pension till his death. His books and teachings attracted a large number of people despite the fact

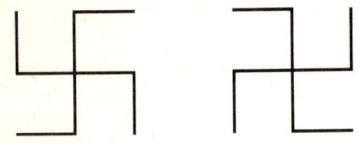

59. Swastikas symbolizing (*a*) good luck, (*b*) ill omen.

sylph

that they were written in Latin and, as such, were beyond the comprehension of the common man. Though many bishops favoured his writings and understood them, the clergy as a whole were hostile. He constantly had visions – one of a great fire, which came true – and his works were translated into all the Scandinavian languages and English. William Blake, the poet, was an admirer and follower. In 1783 a chapel in Sweden was built for the teaching of Swedenborg's doctrines and, though he did not seek to proselytize, there were soon similar chapels throughout the civilized world, each self-governing. His system is rational though mystical and any intelligent person can gain an insight into his beliefs. His aim was to establish a democratic and intelligible church, and his ideas illuminate a great deal of °spiritualism. Altogether he wrote 17 books on his revelations. His interpretations are based on the Bible and reveal much of the true meaning of the Scriptures. Swedenborg studied physiology and anatomy with the intention of finding the °soul. He practised °yoga breathing to produce °ecstasy and this opened the door to °meditation, contemplation and °intuition, and opened a private door to the infinite where he conversed with the spirits of the departed, °angels and °daemons.

sylph. One of a race of °spirits or beings supposed to inhabit the air, including °fairies or fays, brownies, °elves and °pixies. Female sylphs are known as sylphids.

T

table rapping or **tapping.** A method of summoning the departed. Three or more persons sit round a table (usually circular), the tips of their fingers on the surface touching the fingers of the people adjacent. If one (or more) is °sensitive, power is in some way transmitted which enables the sitters to get in touch with °spirits of the departed and communicate with them. Once communication is established, the °spirit is asked to spell out messages, giving one rap for A, two for B, and so on. If questions can be answered by yes or no, then one rap means yes and two mean no. The rapping is done by one leg of the table rising and then falling with an audible rap. The principle is the same as that which actuates the °ouija board. Sometimes °spirits become violent, lift the entire table and toss it about. Table rapping should not be regarded as a parlour game and questions should relate to serious problems the sitters want solved.

tablets of I'sid'i. (Pronounced eeseedee.) Commonly known as the 'squares of Araby' which comprise the °Enochian system of °divination, for according to biblical history Enoch was the first recorder of the °occult arts. The tablets consist of 16 squares across and 16 down, each marked with a symbol. When they are consulted by one who has the key, personal forecasts can be given and solutions to problems found.

taboo, tabu. A Polynesian word meaning set apart or consecrated to a special use or purpose; restricted to the use of a god, king, priest or chief, while forbidden for general use; prohibited to a particular class such as women; inviolable, sacred, forbidden. Taboos connected with animals and plants are a part of °totemism. Taboo restrictions differ from moral or religious prohibitions and the taboo is humanity's oldest unwritten code of law. The violation of a taboo makes the offender taboo. Words and actions can be taboo. The power of taboo is so strong that when those who unwittingly break one and are told what they have done they sometimes suffer convulsions and die of fright. The taboo is one of the ways by which the priests and kings of savage tribes maintain and exercise their power. The power of taboo in South and Central America, Africa, Polynesia, the East and in the West Indies is still extremely potent.

Tagore, Rabindranath (1861–1941). Bengali poet and philosopher born in Calcutta. He was awarded the Nobel Prize for Literature in 1913 and knighted in 1915. He was an ardent practitioner of °yoga and a believer in the °occult. He founded a unique university in Santiniketan which was a microcosm of the world as he wished it to be. He had an immense love and reverence for nature and his students were in constant touch with natural things, which led them to an understanding of the divine. He made work resemble play and every day was a holiday (holy day). Work was for the common good, which made selfish students develop into unselfish ones. Studies were undertaken in a holiday spirit; students did their own cooking and weaving, learnt carpentry, repaired buildings and formed an independent community. Brahmin students who enrolled thinking they were superior to other castes were soon disabused; untouchables who entered shrinking and abasing themselves grew confident and assured. They were taught that love, happiness and compassion were supreme. They learnt that every man is part of every other man and that ultimately

60. Rabindranath Tagore

all will join in harmony and unity. They were taught also to respect their environment. Santiniketan is a prime example of the way in which °yoga should be practised in everyday life and that it is not merely a study for °mystics and anchorites. His writings include *The Golden Boat*, *Late Harvest*, *Dreams* and *Offerings*; °ill. 60.

talisman. Derived from the Arabic *tilsam* (incantation). An object believed to possess magical – usually protective – power for the person possessing or wearing it. Usually a stone, ring or other object engraved with figures to which are attributed the °occult powers of the planetary influences and celestial configurations under which it was made. °Amulets such as the °swastika and °Solomon's seal (or °star) are worn to avert evil or misfortune. Thousands of motorists attach a St Christopher medal to their cars because he is the patron saint of travellers. In 1968 when the US Navy tried to put a number of Vanguard rockets into orbit and failed, the contractors said that failure was caused because they lacked St Christopher medals. One was riveted to the next rocket and it sailed into the stratosphere without mishap.

tantras. °Yoga writings corresponding closely to the *laya-yoga*, a system which lays down special formulae and rituals for the worship of deities (all symbolic) in order to acquire and use powers. The rituals are largely mechanical and repetitive.

tarot. (Pronounced tarot or taro.) The name comes from the Romany word *tar* (pack of cards) and *taurus*. It consists of a double pack of cards, with 78 cards in all. The first pack consists of 22 Major keys each corresponding to a letter of the

 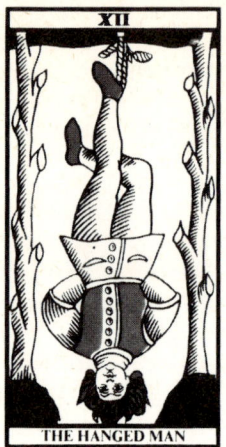 

61. Tarot cards

°mystic Hebrew alphabet; the second consists of 56 Minor keys from which our modern playing cards are derived. Though the Major are more important, a great deal can be learnt from the Minor. The Major Arcanum, as the first pack is called, is much older than the Minor Arcanum. It is not, however, their antiquity that is important but their symbolism. Their allegory and symbolism are catholic, referring to all nations and peoples, many types of ideas and things. According to the late Frank Lind, one of the great British authorities on the tarot, the cards of the Major Arcanum reveal the issues and spiritual truths behind important actions and situations. The Minor cards fill in the details and together the packs form an important source of illumination. Though none can be sure, the tarot is supposed to have originated in Ancient Egypt where the 22 Major Arcanum can be identified with the °Kabalah and the letters of the Hebrew alphabet, for it is known that the Hebrews obtained their mystical knowledge from Egypt. The Major keys were painted on the walls of the initiation temple between 12 columns on each side of the chamber; that is, in each of the 11 spaces between the °lotus pillars. When the Egyptian dynasties were foundering, the knowledge of the tarot was carried east to India and

China, north to Europe and south to Africa. Some say that it was the other way round: the tarot travelled from India to Egypt and that the °gipsies (Egypties) came from the east. The Arabs carried the book to Spain and to this day the cards used for °divination, known as *naibs* (an Egyptian word), are inscribed with the ibis, °pyramids and Egyptian vases. In the Middle Ages the tarot was regarded as a secret cult allied to °witchcraft and there were draconian penalties for all who practised °divination by this means or were found with the cards on them. For this reason the names and illustrations on the cards were changed. The Church and ruling bodies all over Europe banned the tarot, but in Europe it was saved by gamblers. °Divination is only one use for the tarot. The cards contain a wealth of information for those who can truly interpret the symbols and use them; °ill. 61.

tea-leaf reading. A common method of seeing into the future, employed not only by clairvoyants but also by lesser sensitives. The mind impinges on the patterns formed by the dregs at the bottom of the cup and leaves that may have adhered to the sides. These are unconsciously translated into terms relating to people and events in the future. Though unscientific, it often works. In Canada some years ago a policewoman was detailed to trap a woman who read tea cups in a restaurant, but the case was dismissed when the official was compelled under cross-examination to admit that everything the reader had seen in her cup had come to pass.

telegnosis. A form of °telepathy in which a voice is heard.

telekinesis. A term employed in psychical research for the movement of objects by and in the presence of a °medium, apparently without contact, as a result of °occult forces. Some °yogis have demonstrated telekinesis but have consistently refused to submit to tests, as they are indifferent to scientific opinion. In 1966 Dr Ctibor Veseley, lecturer in electrophysiology at the Hradec Kralove University, Czechoslovakia, carried out a number of experiments on apparatus built by Jiri Macku, the department's engineer. This consists of a paper-thin copper disc balanced on a needle on which it can be revolved by an electric motor. The apparatus is housed in a glass-sided non-magnetic case. Sitting 6 feet from it and concentrating his gaze on the disc, Robert Pavlita can make it revolve in the direction he wishes, slow it down or stop it. He has also moved light objects floating on liquid in a predetermined direction by concentrating his will on them. Hundreds of similar experiments are being carried out, some in collaboration with Russian scientists, in order

telepathy

to find out why objects can be made to move when willed to do so, and whether this ability can be developed so that larger and heavier objects, at greater distances, can be moved. Yogis have demonstrated in public, in daylight, that they can raise objects off the ground by will-power. Birgitte Valvanne, wife of a Finnish diplomat, wrote: 'On another occasion, in one of the guest houses of the Birla temples, I saw a holy man lift a chair entirely by will-power. He asked us to assist him by using our will-power. He then gazed intently on the chair and it actually raised itself about two feet into the air, after which it fell to the floor with a crash.' *In Love With India*.

telepathy. Communication by other than known physical means of thoughts, experiences, feelings, etc., from one mind to another, across space, sometimes amounting to thousands of miles. Telepathy is now accepted by scientists as being possible, for there are thousands of authenticated instances of such communication, and distance healing may even be a form of telepathy. The Americans, Russians, British – and perhaps other nations – are trying to harness telepathy for material ends. The Americans, for instance, have a research team at Hanscomb Field, Bedford, USA, consisting of a psychologist, a physicist, an electronics engineer and a mechanical engineer, who have built a computer to test 3 forms of °extra-sensory perception: telepathy, °clairvoyance and precognition. In Leningrad a team, led by Prof. V. Vasilev, is working on telepathy with the intention of communicating with astronauts. In Malaysia Dr Mak Ting Sum (known as Dr Mak), a Fellow of the London College of Physiology and a Member of the Société Internationale de Philologie Sciences, cures diseases, mends broken marriages, helps students to pass examinations and collaborates with the police to trace missing persons – all by telepathy. Celia Green, Director of the Psychophysical Research Unit at Oxford, England, said in 1963 that she and her colleagues were convinced that their research into telepathy could have far-reaching implications for studies of mental health, and the nature and time of dreams.

teleplasm. Hypothetic substances emanating from the body of a °medium and ultimately taking the form of a person.

teleport. The ability to produce °apports solely by exercising the mind.

teleportation. The act or process of transporting objects, humans or animals through space without any mechanical means.

telergy. The supposed or direct action of the mind of one person on the mind of another.

telesthesia. Sensibility to events at a distance.

Tenrikyo. Japanese °psychic movement founded by Miki Nakayama in 1838. She became known as 'mad Miki Nakayama' because she said that God was speaking through her, and attracted a host of followers. Nakayama insisted that the actual site of creation was in Japan and, when challenged to say exactly where, she allowed herself to be blindfolded and walked, stumbling and falling, many miles to a spot which she claimed was the geographical site, called Jiba. As many doubted, she volunteered to repeat the performance and, though on numerous occasions she was taken miles away and blindfolded, she invariably returned to the same spot. 'Here is Shinza,' she said, 'here is Jiba; here is Oyazato, the parents' home.' Thousands who witnessed this example of °second sight believed she had been led by God's hand. Tenrikyo is a fusion of Shinto symbolism, Buddhist manners and Christian ideals. The doctrine is a simple one: all humans are created by God and live by His will. The present head, the Patriarch of Tenrikyo, Elder Nakayama, grandson of the founder, has twice most effectively demonstrated his gift of °second sight. Followers donate a tenth of their earnings to Tenrikyo, which now has numerous educational establishments and facilities.

thaumaturgy. The practice and exercise of °magic.

Thebes, Mme. A famous °seer who lived in France before the First World War and published an almanack which was read by a large number of people. In 1905 she said that an incident in peaceful Belgium would set Europe ablaze; that Germany was threatening Europe in general and France in particular, but she would lose a costly war which would see the end of the Hohenzollerns. She prophesied that the Kaiser would disappear from the scene and Germany would be torn by revolution, massacres and later by another war which she would also lose. On New Year's Day 1899 she said that President Fauré of France would die that year though he seemed in robust health. He died on 16 February 1899. She was fearless in her prophecies and, though occasionally wrong, was so often right that her writings were studied with interest in every embassy in Europe.

theosophy. Sometimes mistakenly called Esoteric Buddhism, the term is derived from the Greek *theos* (god) and *sophia* (wisdom). Forms of philosophic and religious thought which claim a special insight into the divine nature and its constituent movements and processes. India has been the birthplace of most of the theosophical systems based on the *Upanishads*, Vedanta, Samkhya and °yoga.

Theosophical Society. Founded by °Blavatsky and °Olcott in New York in 1875, with °Olcott as President and Blavatsky as Correspondence Secretary. Although °Blavatsky claimed to have °occult powers, she achieved little success in New York, so she and Olcott went to India, where they made a tremendous impact, established a centre in Adyar and became the enemies of the Christian missionaries. They had 3 objects: 1. to form a nucleus of the universal brotherhood of humanity without distinction between race, creed, colour or sex; 2. to promote the study of comparative religion, philosophy and science; 3. to investigate unexplained laws of nature and the powers latent in man. Due mainly to the work of the Theosophical Society, the tenets of Hinduism became known throughout Europe and America and the religion became a thriving, living one and an antidote to Western materialism. Theosophists believe in an eternal God, the life-giver who may not perhaps be heard or seen but can be perceived by the °spirit. Though there are no dogmas, two ideas are generally held: °reincarnation and °karma. Nothing is eternal except God; there is constant change and evolution towards the perfection of man in a state that is known as °nirvana. °Theosophy is extremely popular today when many people are disillusioned and cynical about orthodox religions.

third eye. The Ancient Egyptians represented this in the statues of their gods by a protuberance in the forehead. The °yogis say that the exact location of the third eye is between the eyebrows and the vortex in the centre of the forehead. Symbolically it is triangular in form, is known as the *ajna cakram* and represents eternal knowledge. The power of the third eye is exercised through the thalamus, seat of individual consciousness, and its endocrine glands and nerve connections. Normally the °psychic power of the thalamus works only moderately but when °yoga is practised assiduously and the *cakram* is awakened this eye is opened. It is not in any sense a physical eye, but when concentration and °meditation have been mastered, and a state of *samadhi* (a form of deep, self-induced anaesthesia) achieved, the °subconscious mind opens, laying bare all its previous records, and evil impressions are removed. When ignorance has been swept away, °intuition, which can penetrate the thickest veil, can work without interruption. The third eye is probably the pineal gland but it cannot come into operation without the aid of the thalamus and the full development of the *ajna cakram*. Any ambition to develop the third eye in order to become a °medium for gain or other material purpose is supposed to result in failure.

Thompson, K.J. (1935–). Publisher of *Yoga*, the official quarterly of the movement in Britain.

thought. The process of thinking; the faculty of reason; consideration.

thought form. °Tulpa.

thought photography. Based on the theory that °thoughts, which consist of °vibrations, are material and like all material objects leave impressions. °Serios is a recent example of a subject whose thoughts can be photographed; °de la Warr was another who produced successful photographs of projected thoughts. The earliest pioneer in this field was probably Prof. Fukari, a Japanese, who conducted thought-photography sessions in his home with friends. These were so successful that the editor of *Ube Daily* hired the Arakawa Theatre and in the presence of a large audience produced a dozen dry plates, with the seals unbroken, that had been bought locally. Four images were suggested to the °medium, Koichi Mita, who took only 1 minute to impress them on the plates by gazing into the lens. Further public demonstrations, often witnessed by more than 1,000 people, took place over a period of years. Not all were uniformly successful. In 1928 Prof. Fukari, accompanied by Dr Kenichi Yamamoto, a spiritual healer, visited London and during a seance on 19 September they impregnated a number of plates solely by thought; °spirit photography.

thought reading. The apprehension by one individual of the °thoughts that are passing through the mind of another, though sometimes vast distances may separate them. Occasionally this ability is brought about by interference with the mechanism of the brain. An instance of this occurred in 1917 when Dr Franz Polgar, a Hungarian lieutenant, was knocked unconscious by an explosion. On regaining consciousness in hospital he realized he had acquired the uncanny ability to read the thoughts of the doctors and nurses, and he told them exactly what they were thinking. His extraordinary faculty was reported to the German intelligence agency, which tried to make him read the minds of captured submarine commanders and field officers, but they failed to exploit his gift because his hatred of the Germans set up a mental block through which °thoughts could not penetrate. After the war he went to America where he demonstrated his thought-reading ability at New York University; °twins.

thought transference. °Telepathy.

Thouless, Dr R.H. (1894–). Reader in Psychology at Cambridge University, who was one of a committee set up under the terms of the Perrott Scholarship in Psychical Research, established at Trinity College as a memorial to F.W.

62. Totem poles carved by Haida Indians on the Thunder Bird Park, Victoria, British Columbia

°Myers. He and Dr B.P. Wiesner, a biochemist, made extensive researches into °extra-sensory perception and divided it into 2 types which they called ESP (incoming and cognitive) and PK (motor or outgoing). They decided that the nucleus of the individual or self is the °soul, which learns about impacts on the senses by ESP and controls the body's motor activity by PK. Extra-sensory perception by-passes the sense organs altogether. *The Psi Process in Normal and 'Paranormal' Psychology*, Thouless and Wiesner.

time. A fundamental directional aspect of experience based on the direct experience of the protensity (duration) of sensation and on the experience of change from one sensory event, idea or train of °thought to another, and distinguishing in experience beginning, middle and end, as well as past, present and future. In the material world there is constant change, so for practical purposes we relate change to time and space, which are really abstractions without independent reality. Time is used for convenience to represent changes. Though there is a continuous succession of changes and times, this does not mean that time is continuous. To speak of infinite time is meaningless and, in fact, incomprehensible to the normal mind. In the present, which exists for a fraction of a second, the past is no more and the future has not arrived. Past, present and future are, therefore, merely relative to each other.

totemism. The system of law and custom centring round the totem as a social and religious institution; °ill. 62.

trance. A bodily and mental condition which can be induced at will by some people, usually °mediums, or which may be induced in others, during which a state of abnormal mental perception is attained. There are many and varied types of trance. That which is manifested by mediums on spiritualistic platforms is usually light, the medium in most instances being conscious of everything that is said by or through him. The trance state for psychical phenomena, direct voice or deep trance control, is entirely different. The °medium induces it at will; breathing is deeper and slower, the pulse grows weaker, and the medium seems to lapse into °unconsciousness. The body is then controlled by a °spirit entity, speaking with its own voice, often in a foreign tongue, and displaying knowledge well outside the range of the medium. Experiments have proved that, in this condition, the medium's body is in a state of suspended animation. A deep trance may last for 6–8 hours without the slightest ill effect on the °medium when he regains consciousness. A third type of trance is pro-

transmigration

duced under °hypnosis, which will vary according to the controlling hypnotist and the treatment required. Major surgical operations have been conducted under °hypnosis, the patient talking and even eating and drinking, but being unaware of what has taken place after being brought round. No attempt should be made to go into a state of trance or induce it in others except under the supervision of an expert medium or hypnotist; °hypnotism; °psychic surgery.

transmigration. The passage of the °soul at death into another body, often confused with °reincarnation. °Metempsychosis. Transmigration buttresses the theory of heredity in which physical features or traits are handed down, whereas in °reincarnation the person either changes sex or takes on the characteristics of the opposite sex.

tulpa. °Thought form, which becomes human through the agency of °ghosts or °daemons which can remain at large for years once it has evolved; mischievous puppet with the vitality to possess humans and inert objects.

tumo. A Tibetan word meaning heat; not ordinary heat, but mysterious heat self-engendered by anchorites. There are 3 kinds of tumo: 1. exotic, which arises spontaneously from raptures and envelops the mystic in 'the soft, warm mantle of the gods'; 2. esoteric, which keeps hermits snug on snowy hills; 3. mystic, for which warmth is merely a figurative term and is really an experience of heavenly bliss in this world. °David-Neel says that after a long period of probation, during which she practised breathing and °meditation, she was told to bathe in an icy mountain stream, then, without drying her body or dressing, to spend the night motionless and in °meditation at an altitude of 10,000 feet. After that she became immune to cold, renounced all woollen or fur clothing and never approached a fire to warm herself. Training for tumo is never practised inside a house or near habitations, because foul air and smells produced by smoke impede progress. Tumo is an adaptation of °yoga practice and Mt Everest expeditions have often reported seeing naked men meditating on snow-clad hills at altitudes well above 10,000 feet. Once tumo has been mastered pride, anger, hatred, covetousness, sloth and stupidity melt away. The mind sharpens to gain °intuition and perception, and the body becomes immune to disease. Death results from the natural process of deterioration of the organs.

Turner, Gordon (1924–1975). Born of a Welsh mother and Scots father, both he and his brother, Geoffrey, were °psychic. He was co-founder of the National Federation of Spiritual Healers and was a Life Honorary

Twigg

63. Gordon Turner

Vice-President. He was a healer from childhood but did not become a full-time professional till 1949. He read psychology and sociology at London University, was a book critic, lecturer and playwright, and made several TV appearances in connection with spiritual healing. He made 2 long-playing records, 'Meditation' and 'Sleep'. The Gordon Turner Healing Centre has been established in London, where a room is set aside for animal patients because he believed in the 'oneness of life'. He served in the RAF and, though badly injured in action and blind for a time, could always 'see from within'. Later his sight was restored. He studied Zen under a Tibetan monk and conducted research in various fields of the °occult, such as photography of the °aura. The brain, he thought, limits our acceptance of the invisible world and °meditation may open the door; °ill. 63.

Twigg, Ena (1914–). Born in Kent, England, of a Welsh mother and English father. The entire family – parents and 4 children – was °psychic. At the age of 7 she used to see 'misty people', with whom she spoke and played, and at 14 they told her that her father would die 'a week from today'. After her marriage to Harry Twigg both were disturbed by her °second sight. Her life was transformed when she fell seriously ill. Doctors could do nothing for her, but 3 visitors from the °spirit world, visible only to her, gave assurances that she would be restored to health. After one had given her an injection in the neck she gradually improved and, out of gratitude, she decided to devote her life to helping others. She joined the Marylebone Spiritualist Association (now the °Spiritualist Association of Great Britain) and later set up an independent healing clinic. She is a mental °medium, a °trance medium, clairaudient, clairvoyant, a diagnostician and a spiritual healer. Her purpose in life is to prove that there is an existence after physical death. Her many and varied experiences are recorded in *Ena Twigg – Medium*,

twins, identical

64. Ena Twigg

her autobiography written in collaboration with Ruth Hagy Brod; °clairaudience; °clairvoyance; °ill. 64.

twins, identical. According to °astrology babies born within minutes of each other, who look, act and think alike, are known as identical twins, and bear out the theory that people born at the same place and almost exactly at the same time will think and act alike, and will have careers that run parallel. Scores of instances prove this theory and there are innumerable recorded instances of such twins committing the same acts and thinking the same °thoughts though separated by thousands of miles. Twins are not all identical; 1 pair was born 56 days apart in Sydney, Australia.

Tyrrell, G. M. N. (1879–1952). A pioneer radio engineer who, before the First World War, introduced radio into Mexico. He was interested in psychical research and in 1923 decided to devote his life to investigating the mind and the unknown. His best-known books are *Science and Psychical Phenomena*, *The Personality of Man*, and *Apparitions*. He joined the °Society for Psychical Research in 1908 and was elected President in 1945. Few did more to raise psychical research from the realms of °magic and °superstition to its present level.

U

unconscious. One of the 4 states of awareness. In psychology the unconscious is best understood as the aggregate of the dynamic elements constituting the personality, some of which the individual may be aware of as part of his make-up, of others entirely unaware. Few people realize the reasons for their actions and desires; most people imagine that they control their own destinies. Many of the acts we perform, however, are due to underlying forces of which we have no cognizance and which are born in the unconscious mind. When cosmic ignorance – the failure to understand life and its purpose, and the inability to distinguish between the permanent and the transitory – has been abolished, first by concentration and then by °meditation, the unconscious can be brought to the surface; °conscious; °Freud; °Jung; °subconscious; °superconscious.

undine. Nymph or female water sprite; one of the embodiments of the 4 elements: °sylph, °gnome, undine and °salamander, including oceanides and nereides of the sea.

V

vampire. Derived from the Magyar *vampir*; a malignant creature believed to be a reanimated corpse who seeks nourishment by sucking the blood of sleeping persons. Belief in vampires was widely held in the Middle Ages throughout South-East Europe, especially in Russia, Bohemia and Hungary. It was believed that after death bodies: 1. decayed till only the skeleton remained; 2. if the deceased was very holy his body preserved its natural colour and consistency for an indefinite period and gave off a pleasant odour; 3. if the person had been excommunicated or was an undetected murderer or a suicide, his body turned black, swelled like a balloon and stank abominably. It was to this third category that vampires belonged. They were supposed to rise from the grave every night except on Fridays, steal into homes and suck the blood of those who slept. The only protection during sleep was to hang garlic over the bed. In 1846 Walter Mapes gave examples of vampirism in England during the 12th century, and vampirism is supposed to have reached its peak in Southern Europe during the early 18th century. One explanation given by occultists is that a vampire is the °astral body or °etheric double of a dead person who sometimes may be seen as a °phantom, but there is no authenticated evidence of the existence of vampires.

Van Pelt, Dr S. J., MB, BS, (1908–   ). Former President of the British Society of Medical Hypnotists; editor of the *British Journal of Medical Hypnotism*; a member of the BMA, the National Association for Mental Health, the Society for Clinical and Experimental Hypnosis (New York), and the Society for the Study of Addiction to Alcohol and other Drugs. Dr Van Pelt, a pioneer in the field of therapeutic °hypnosis, author of 6 books on the subject and co-author of 3, had a specialist practice in London. He has lectured widely, subscribed numerous articles to scientific journals on °hypnotism and has been largely instrumental in elevating it into a scientific study.

vibrations. All matter consists of vibrations, which oscillate at varying rates per second, known as cycles. Breathing, sight, °colour, noise and music – even °thought – are vibrations in different forms. °Yoga breathing, for instance, is based on the theory of vibrations, recognized in the West only within the last century. During *pranayama* these are generated in the lower part of the spine; then as technique develops and is mastered, the vibrations ascend till they reach the brain, giving supranormal powers which should never be harnessed to base ends, otherwise they will destroy the subject. °Mantras and °thoughts of every kind are based on the theory that certain words and phrases, if enunciated in the correct way, affect both body and mind, creating sorrow, ecstasy, fear and other emotions. Thoughts generated by concentration can bend metal objects and can travel over vast distances to affect others for good or evil. Most people are affected in their everyday life by the vibrations of music, poetry, eloquent speech, the incessant roar of cars, road drills, etc., which are either helpful or harmful. Vibrations are made use of by all great religions to bring worshippers and others under control, and to engender respect and reverence. Hypnotic effects are also achieved by vibrations through the power of the eye and mind. Healing may be achieved by vibrations which emanate from the finger-tips. In the past all such power was labelled as °magic, but now science has an explanation for some types of vibrations and has harnessed them (e.g. X-rays, ultrasonics and lasers) to heal and sometimes to destroy.

vision. Something that is apparently seen otherwise than by ordinary sight; an appearance of a prophetic or mystical character, or having the nature of a revelation, supernaturally presented to the mind in sleep, or in an abnormal state.

voodoo, vaudoux, hoodoo. Derived from the West African (Dahomey) *vodu*, meaning superstitious beliefs and practices involving °sorcery, °serpent worship, and sacrificial rites prevalent among Negroes and the descendants of Negroes in West Africa, the West Indies and the southern states of the USA. Voodoo has taken a firm hold in Haiti where the population is mainly Negro with a mixture of white blood. The people speak Creole, a French dialect, and their religion is an admixture of Roman Catholicism and West African, and the ritual has degenerated into a form of voodoo. Blood rites are indulged in under the crucifix, the °Black Mass is chanted and °sacrifices of young animals and even children are made. The Voodoo Church appoints bishops, priests and priestesses who take part in ritual dances. Among the phenomena experienced is that of °obsession where a member of the community falls into a °trance, is vested with power and proclaimed a god. He walks to the sacrificial altar, partakes of freshly killed food and blood, makes °prophecies to the accompaniment of chanted hymns and then falls into a deep sleep before eventually returning to normality. Though voodoo is frowned on by all the great religions there is little doubt that it has the power to sway and terrify the ignorant and superstitious, and to produce phenomena for which science can in no way account. George Kelly, who led an expedition into the hinterland of Haiti, revealed (*Sunday Chronicle* 10 June 1934) that an increasing number of whites in the country are ardent practitioners of voodoo. 'A gruesome practice,' he says, 'is to dig up a corpse and dress the body in the clothes of their enemy. Within the space of a day or two the enemy will be taken ill, grow rapidly worse and eventually die.' Kelly and his party investigated the case of a voodoo °witch doctor who undertook to turn a black man white. He was made to drink a concoction, incantations were repeated over him and within a day or two his skin peeled and he was many shades lighter.

W

Wagner, Edward A. (1906–). Born in Philadelphia, USA, he became a reporter on the *Cleveland Press*, where he worked with Harry Houdini, famous magician and escapologist, first in exposing spiritualistic frauds and charlatan °seers, then on a series to expose °astrology, which transformed Wagner from a scoffer into a believer. He was associated with various °occult and astrological groups, among them the °Rosicrucians for whom he lectured and taught and became Assistant Superintendent of Publications. He founded his own astrological publishing company, was editor of the *National Astrological Journal* for 3 years and syndicated articles on °astrology throughout America. In 1945 Wagner married Julia Coppa and between them they produce *Horoscope*, the world's leading astrological magazine, and a score of allied publications.

warlock. The °Devil or one in league with the °Devil, thus possessing °occult and evil powers; sorcerer; wizard; °witch.

werwolf, werewolf. According to medieval mythology, a person who was transformed or was capable of transforming himself into a wolf. In ancient times the belief was widely held and there are many instances of men being killed or tortured because they were accused of being werwolves, one of the best known being that of Giles Garnier of Lyons, who in 1573 was charged at Dole and under torture confessed that he had changed himself into a wolf and in that guise had killed, torn to pieces and partly eaten a 12-year-old girl. In Germany and France °witches were accused of changing into once-sacred goats; in Britain the favoured beasts were bulls, dogs and cats. A belief in werwolves dies hard and as recently as 1925 a policeman in a Rhineland village shot a boy who was suspected of being one. Today we realize that werwolves are the victims of a mental disorder known as °lycanthropy, in which the afflicted imagines that he is a wolf or some other wild animal, and tries to act like one; °leopard men; °wolf-men.

whirling dervish. °Dervish.

witch. A female magician or sorceress dealing either in white or °black magic. A white witch helps people who are suffering or distressed and tries to relieve their condition. A black witch deals with the °Devil or with evil °spirits and through their agency performs supernatural acts. A belief in witches has existed since the dawn of civilization and, though Charlemagne banned the burning of witches in the 9th century, 400 years later they were still being persecuted. A witch mania spread through Germany and 100,000 women lost their lives in the reign of terror. In Salem, USA, in the winter of 1691–1692, several hundred women and girls were arrested for practising °witchcraft and 19 were hanged. By 1720 public opinion had so changed that a Boston man charged with °witchcraft had his accuser convicted for defamation of character and in 1735 the British Parliament declared that 'witches do not exist'. Belief in witchcraft persists all over the world and is, for instance, a flourishing cult in Bihar, India, where it is practised by the Adibasis tribe in Chotanagpur. A recent survey in America showed that there are 225,000 minor and 260 major witches in the country, among them 2 Congressmen, several high-ranking military officers and 1 famous television personality. Britain also has its °covens; °ill. 65.

witchcraft. The practices of a °witch or °witch doctor; the exercise of supernatural power supposed to be possessed by persons in league with the °Devil or evil °spirits. Exercise of the °magic arts, good or bad; bewitching or fascinating by means of °charms, °amulets, °spells or potions. Witchcraft probably originated in prehistoric times and has certainly flourished throughout the world. Fundamentalists condemn witchcraft out of hand, for Exodus 22:18 says, 'Thou shalt not suffer a witch to live.' Later (1 Samuel 29:7), 'Then, said Saul unto his servants, Seek me a woman that hath a familiar spirit, that I may go unto her and inquire of her. And his servants said unto him, Behold there is a woman that hath a familiar spirit at En-dor.' Because witchcraft delved into the unknown, it was feared and °witches were burnt at the stake or hanged and quartered.

witch doctor. One who professes to cure disease and to counteract witchcraft by °magic. Generally considered to flourish only in West Africa, chiefly the Congo, but in fact they practise in Melanesia, Polynesia, among the °Aborigines of Australia, the North American Indians, in Haiti, in South and Central America, India and South-East Asia under different names. There are good as well as evil witch-doctors: the good comfort, help and cure; the evil cast °spells which bring misfortune, illness and even death. The best of the good witch-doctors are always more powerful

65. 19th-century representation of a witch on a broomstick

wolf-men

66. A witch-doctor in the Northern Territory of Australia shows how the magic bone is pointed at a victim while he is being 'sung'. Although the ceremony is performed in secret, the victim learns of it and, among the tribal people, usually dies.

than those who practise evil; °ill. 66.

wolf-men. N. American Indians, such as the Ojibway on the reservation at Pickerel, Ontario, will never kill a wolf except as a desperate measure of self-defence, for they believe wolves to be the earthly disguise of a celestial people, the °reincarnation of ancient warriors. It is said that on dark nights when none can see them, wolves rear on their hind legs, their snouts shorten, their legs lengthen and their hair creeps up to the top of their heads; they are then transformed into savage men, the deadly foes of lonely travellers. Witnesses have stated that they have seen wolf-men chase frantic deer on to lonely station platforms, and kill and devour them under the startled eyes of waiting passengers. No real wolf would do such a thing. Wolfmen, so the superstitious say, howl outside churches on Christmas Eve and on Christmas night; they follow hearses and funeral corteges, but

147

are far too wily for the police or even the Mounties, for they wait till the nights are black and the moon and stars demand blood; °leopard men; °werwolf.

Woodruff, Maurice (?–1973). Son of a famous clairvoyant who inherited her gift. He called himself 'a clairvoyant and astrologer', but his powers were obviously clairvoyant, for no astrologer has the ability to make snap °predictions as he did. His °predictions, which were 80 per cent accurate, were often made on public platforms, before large audiences in TV studios or theatres, about people he had never seen. In this he differed from many of his kind who insist on darkened rooms, freedom from distractions and an atmosphere conducive to the summoning of °spirits. There is no scientific explanation for his powers, other than that he possessed an extraordinary degree of °extra-sensory perception. He publicly made some astonishingly accurate predictions about Lord Snowdon, Elizabeth Taylor, Donald Campbell, whose death he predicted, and President John F. Kennedy and his brother, whom he 'saw' would be assassinated, as well as many other household figures. He died from a heart attack in Singapore; °clairvoyance.

Wright, Dr Harry B. A dental surgeon and a member of the Explorers' Club, USA. After hearing a paper presented by Dr H.F. Dunbar on 'Emotions and Bodily Change' in 1951, he went to the Congo to look for a °witch doctor to confirm Dunbar's thesis. The outcome was *Witness To Witchcraft*, one of the best authenticated books on the subject. He found that there is a remarkable similarity in the methods of °witch doctors and psychoanalysts in America, a fact already noted by Dr Charles Pidoux, a French psychiatrist who had studied the mental healing practices of °witch doctors in the Niger. Later he made journeys into the hinterland of Africa, South America and Oceania for the same purpose, and his valuable contributions have added to those of travellers, anthropologists and researchers in this field.

Wulff, Wilhelm. A painter, sculptor and astrologer who, during the purge that followed Hess's flight to Scotland during the Second World War, was arrested by the Gestapo and sent to a concentration camp. He was released on condition that he would work as an astrologer for SS leaders and cast the °horoscopes of Kersten, Schellenberg, Nebe and Himmler. He was given the necessary data on Hitler and predicted that he would not be assassinated. He told Himmler that Germany would lose the war. An account of his experiences is given in *Zodiac and Swastika*; °astrology.

X

xenoglossia. Knowledge by a person of a language he has never learned. It occurs in religious °ecstasy, under °hypnosis, in °trance by a °medium and in certain pathological states. George Valantine, the American °medium, was used by the voice of Confucius who spoke in archaic Chinese, a language unknown to Valentine. He also spoke in other foreign tongues, though he had but an elementary education; his normal conversation was halting and his flow of ideas limited; °Eddy family; °glossolalia.

Y

yang and yin. The dual expressions of Ch'i, the motivating force behind all life, which enters the body at birth. According to the Chinese, all matter is made of yin and yang, the undefinable and invisible force of life, which leaves at death. During lifetime it flows in a continuous pattern along a system of channels and, if thrown out of equilibrium, the body falls ill. They correspond to the *nadis*, or vital airs in °yoga.

Yeats-Brown, D.F.C. (1886–1944). Soldier, journalist and °mystic, he was the son of Montague Yeats-Brown, British Consul-General in Genoa, educated at Harrow and Sandhurst, and served in the Royal Rifle Corps and 17th Cavalry, Indian Army. He retired in 1925 and became assistant editor of the London *Spectator* and was author of *Lives Of A Bengal Lancer*. He travelled widely in India, Canada, USA and Europe, and wrote and lectured on °yoga and Indian mysticism. He did, perhaps, more than anyone by magazine articles, books and lectures to popularize the study of °yoga in Britain and America; °ill. 67.

Yesudian, Selvarajan. He is the author of *A Yoga Miscellany* and, in collaboration with Elizabeth Haich, of *Yoga and Destiny* and *Yoga and Health*. He is a recognized living

Yi King

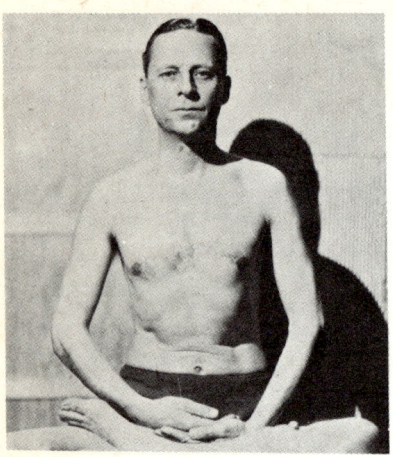

67. D.F.C. Yeats-Brown

authority on *hatha-yoga* and a pioneer of this art in Europe, where he and Haich opened a school for enthusiasts in Switzerland; °yoga.

Yi King. (Pronounced yee ching.) I Ching. One of the oldest forms of °divination, the use of which is first recorded by Fu Hsi, in 3222 BC. When King Wan, founder of the Han dynasty, was taken prisoner by the King of Yin and incarcerated at Ho Nan he spent his entire time meditating and analysing the Yi King and its 64 hexagrams. As a result of his deliberations he produced the present form of °prediction. Yi King is an abstruse study. Confucius said that, if he had his life over again, he would devote 50 years to the study of Yi King in order to unravel its mysteries and understand them fully. Originally there were 3 books devoted to *Yee*: *Lien Shan*, *Zang* and *Yi King*. The first 2 were burnt by an edict of the King of Zin, who destroyed all books and manuscripts with the exception of Yi King and the works of his own scholars. Yi King was saved only because it was indispensable as the prime work on °divination and contained the key to the solution of the many problems which constantly arose. The Yi King has been translated only 4 times: into Latin by Regius and the Roman Catholic missionaries between the 15th and 16th centuries; in 1854 into English by Prof. James Legge; in 1876 by Canon McClatchie; in 1972 by Alfred Douglas, *The Oracle of Change: How To Consult the I-Ching*; °ill. 68.

yin. One of the dual expressions of Ch'i; °yang.

yoga. Derived from the Sanskrit *yog* (union). Refers to a state in which thought and action are in complete harmony, and is applied by the Hindus to any system by means of which it is believed that the °soul may be emancipated from the *maya* (illusion) of Earth-life and attain union with *ishvara* (universal soul). Eight stages are laid down for the practice of yoga by Hindu philosophers: 1. *yama*, restraint, forbearance; 2. *niyama*, religious observances; 3. *asana*, posture; 4. *pranayama*, control of breath; 5. *pratyhara*,

Upper Trigram → Lower Trigram ↓	Ch'ien ☰	Chên ☳	K'an ☵	Kên ☶	K'un ☷	Sun ☴	Li ☲	Tui ☱
Ch'ien ☰	1	4	5	26	11	9	14	43
Chên ☳	25	51	3	27	24	42	21	17
K'an ☵	6	40	29	4	7	59	64	47
Kên ☶	33	62	39	52	15	53	56	31
K'un ☷	12	16	8	23	2	20	35	45
Sun ☴	44	32	48	18	46	57	50	28
Li ☲	13	55	63	22	36	37	30	49
Tui ☱	10	54	60	41	19	61	38	58

Key to the construction of the hexagrams

Name	Attribute	Image	Family Relationship
Ch'ien ☰ the Creative	strong	heaven	father
K'un ☷ the Receptive	devoted, yielding	earth	mother
Chên ☳ the Arousing	inciting movement	thunder	first son
K'an ☵ the Abysmal	dangerous	water	second son
Kên ☶ Keeping Still	resting	mountain	third son
Sun ☴ the Gentle	penetrating	wind wood	first daughter
Li ☲ the Clinging	light-giving	fire	second daughter
Tui ☱ the Joyous	joyful	lake	third daughter

68. The various combinations of the wooden pieces used in Yi King

yoga philosophy

restraint of the senses; 6. *dharana*, calming the mind by concentration; 7. *dhyana*, abstract contemplation; 8. *samadhi*, ecstatic °meditation. No reasons are given for some of the practices by which one attains ultimate union, as these are based on the results of trial and error over a period of centuries. The *chela* (disciple) has only to adhere faithfully to the discipline and results will follow; °yogi.

yoga philosophy. One of the 6 Hindu systems for the development of the soul, the others being *nyana, vaisesika, samkhya* (or *sankhya*), *purva mimamsa* and *vedanta*.

yogi. A male who practises °yoga.

yogini. A female who practises °yoga.

Young, Brigham (1801–1877). After the assassination of °Smith, founder of the Latter-Day Saints, Young was unanimously accepted as his successor. On 14 January 1847 he had a revelation from the Lord in which he was told to lead his people west to what is now Salt Lake City, 'the promised land'. They cultivated the fertile soil but, when the harvest was ready, swarms of crickets settled and started to devour the crops. In desperation Young and his followers fell on their knees and asked the Lord to intervene, at which clouds of gulls swooped in from the mountains and devoured the insects. In gratitude for this miracle a monument surmounted by a sea-gull was erected in Temple Square, Salt Lake City. Under the guidance of Young and a council of 12 apostles, the Mormons, who now number 12 million, have grown rich and prosperous, and have spread their gospel throughout the world. Originally, because the Old Testament teaches that the patriarchs had more than 1 wife, polygamy was sanctioned, but in the 1880s Congress forbade this and today adultery is considered next in gravity to murder. A sacred concept is attached to the human body and, as it is a sin to injure the body and dissipate health, the use of alcohol, tobacco, drugs and other deleterious substances is discouraged; °ill. 69.

69. Brigham Young

Z

Zadkiel I, the Seer (1795–1874). Captain James Richard Morrison, RN, resigned from the Royal Navy in 1829 and devoted the remainder of his life to °astrology and invention. In 1831 he published *Herald of Astrology* and in 1832 *Zadkiel's Almanac* in which he made predictions for the following year. From the start the latter had an annual sale of more than 60,000 copies. He was the first important modern British astrological °seer; °Zadkiel II.

Zadkiel II (1840–1923). Alfred John Pearce was a scientist, astrologer and author of many textbooks on °astrology. His 'Pearce Theory' is still followed by many. He was a pupil of Zadkiel I, a friend and associate of W.T. Stead and the Hon. Ralph Shirley, editor of *Occult Review*, and a keen student of Egyptology. After Morrison's death, he took over the publication of his *Zadkiel's Almanac* and sent the circulation up to 200,000. He and Morrison sought to place °astrology on a scientific basis and cut away much of the °superstition with which it had been encumbered after the death of men like °Lilly, °Dee and °Culpepper; °Zadkiel I, the Seer.

Zarathustra (500–400 BC). The founder of Zoroastrianism, he was supposed to have been miraculously conceived by his mother when she was 15. His life is in many ways similar to that of Christ: his life was threatened by a Turanian prince, the Herod of his day; he retired to the mountains for °meditation and was led into the presence of God by an archangel, where he received a revelation; he was tempted by Angra Mainyu, the Lord of Evil. Unlike Christ, Zarathustra was never regarded as a °reincarnation of the Deity, but simply as a great prophet. There are 2 schools of Zoroastrianism: those who follow his original teachings, and those who follow the character and achievements of Zoroaster the Magician, whose language was Aramaean. The latter school is interested mainly in °astrology, for Zoroaster (Zarathustra) was reputed to be a magus, a thaumaturgist, that is a miracle worker, and a °mystic. What little is known of him is set down in the °*Zend-Avesta*, the sacred scriptures of Zoroastrianism, and in the *Pahlivi* books. There are also references to him in oriental scrolls written in Syrian, Iranian and

153

Arabic, and a legendary account of his life exists in *Zartusht Naman*, published in the 13th century. Greek and Roman historians wrote about him; Aristotle was familiar with his teachings, and Pliny the Elder, Apuleius the novelist, and the Church fathers, Lactantius and Clement, mentioned him frequently. In the °*Zend-Avesta* he was called Zarathrustra and it was the Greeks who called him Zoroaster. Details of his personal life appear in the 5 *Gathas*, which resemble the *Upanishads* of the Hindus and consist of a miscellaneous collection of prayers, hymns and instructions, and references to his family and contain 2 complete chapters on the nature of the Deity. None of the tenets of Zoroastrianism conflict with those of other great religions. At the age of 30, after 10 years of preaching compassion, the benefits of agriculture and home building, he had gained only 1 disciple; by the age of 42 he was a power in the land with thousands of converts. He preceded Christ, Buddha and °Mahomet and, as his influence extended throughout the Arab world, his ideas may have influenced all 3. He believed that the elements must be kept free from defilement. Today boys in the Parsee schools in Bombay, who are ethnically the descendants of Iranian °Zoroastrians, begin their morning around a burning brazier, with a prayer to the °sun. They also turn to the °sun, symbol of life, when they pray. The rites laid down by Zarathustra are still followed by the Gabars of Iran who live near Zazd, though oddly enough these are tinged with an acquired Hindu flavour.

Zend-Avesta. The scriptures of the °Zoroastrians.

zener cards. Are so-called after the name of their inventor. There are 5 cards bearing simple diagrams. A pack consists of 50 with 10 of each kind. They were first used in large-scale experiments by Prof. J. B. °Rhine and others engaged in testing precognition; °Soal; °ill. 70.

70. Zener cards

Zimbabwe Acropolis

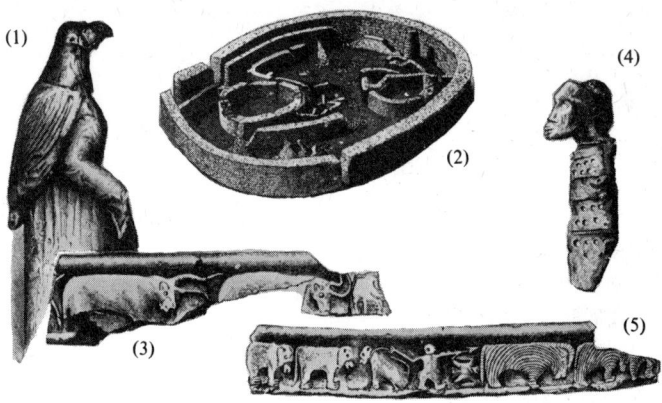

71. Antiquities of Zimbabwe, from a plate published in 1892: (1) Vulture's head; (2) Model of ruins; (3) oxen; (4) head of man; (5) hunt.

Zimbabwe Acropolis. No one knows who conceived and designed this great acropolis, a vast stone monument in Rhodesia, though it was undoubtedly built by local labour. Fragments of Chinese, Persian and Arab porcelain and glass have been discovered on and beneath its original floor, and the symbols on a wooden bowl found on the site have given rise to controversy. Prof. McIver, Miss Caton-Thompson and Prof. Leo Frobenius, the German savant, maintain that it is a relic of an empire which flourished some 3,000 years ago and extended over much of Southern Africa. Dr Nazaroff said in 1931 that the remains of the towers in Zimbabwe resemble the Towers of Silence of the °Zoroastrians, and Karl Mauch that they resemble the Temple of King Solomon on Mt Moriah and the palace inhabited by the Queen of Sheba. Local °witch doctors throw 64 pieces of carved bone called *hakata* when they predict, which bear a strong similarity to the 64 hexagrams of the °Yi King; but carvings on the bones also link them with Ancient Egypt and medieval England. From what little we know, the people who inhabited Zimbabwe were highly civilized and deeply interested in the °occult; °ill. 71.

zodiac. In astronomy a belt of celestial spheres extending 8 or 9 degrees on each side of the ecliptic, within which the apparent motions of the sun, moon and principal planets take place. As this is the Earth's

155

zodiacal constellations

magnetic field, astrologers believe that all human beings are affected in varying degrees by the planets. The zodiac is divided into 12 equal parts called the signs. There are 2 zodiacs: 1. the actual zodiac of the constellations; 2. the conventional one used in astronomy and °astrology; °signs of the zodiac.

zodiacal constellations. The path through which the sun, moon and stars appear to move. The sun takes 1 year and the moon 28 days to complete a circuit of the Earth, while the planets take varying periods. This °zodiac is not used in astronomy but is the base for astrological calculations; °astrology; °horoscope; °signs of the zodiac; °zodiac.

zombie. A corpse said to be resuscitated by means of °witchcraft and made to work, usually on a plantation, at simple, routine and monotonous duties without payment or reward. Zombies have neither intelligence nor feeling and act like robots, obeying the will of their masters. A belief in zombies is rife throughout the West Indies, Central and South America and in parts of West Africa, though the practice of reviving and keeping them as slaves seems to be restricted to Haiti, where it is banned by law. The existence of zombies has been questioned, but Zora Houston claims in her book *Voodoo Gods* to have seen a zombie named Felicia Felix-Mentor in a hospital yard in Haiti. She writes: 'I had the rare opportunity of seeing and touching an authentic case. I listened to the broken noises in its throat, and then I did what no one else has done: I photographed it. If I had not experienced all this in strong sunlight, in a hospital yard, I might have come away from Haiti interested but doubtful. But I saw this case of Felicia Felix-Mentor, which was vouched for on the highest authority. So I know that there are zombies in Haiti.' According to Houston there are various reasons for bringing back the dead: one was brought back to life because he was wanted as a beast of burden, another was reduced to the level of a beast as an act of revenge; there are also other reasons. Sometimes these people know that they will be resurrected before they die. Bocors or °voodoo specialists who bring the dead back to life are said to exist also in the southern states of the USA, where plantation owners used to pay bocors to create zombies to work for them as free labour. This is done by a secret ritual and °black magic.

Zoroaster. The name by which °Zarathustra was known to the Greeks.

Zoroastrian. A follower of the teachings of °Zoroaster; since 1811, a Parsee. There are more than 150,000 Parsees scattered throughout India, most of them in the Bombay presidency; °Zarathustra.